The Divining Rod

DEPARTMENT OF THE INTERIOR
FRANKLIN K. LANE, 'Secretary

UNITED STATES GEOLOGICAL SURVEY
GEORGE OTIS SMITH, Director

Water-Supply Paper 416

THE DIVINING ROD

A HISTORY OF WATER WITCHING

WITH A BIBLIOGRAPHY

BY

ARTHUR J. ELLIS

WASHINGTON
GOVERNMENT PRINTING OFFICE
1917

ADDITIONAL COPIES
OF THIS PUBLICATION MAY BE PROCURED FROM
THE SUPERINTENDENT OF DOCUMENTS
GOVERNMENT PRINTING OFFICE
WASHINGTON, D. C.
AT
10 CENTS PER COPY

CONTENTS.

ILLUSTRATIONS.

INTRODUCTORY NOTE.

By O. E. Meinzer.

The use of a forked twig, or so-called divining rod, in locating minerals, finding hidden treasure, or detecting criminals is a curious superstition that has been a subject of discussion since the middle of the sixteenth century and still has a strong hold on the popular mind, even in this country, as is shown by the large number of inquiries received each year by the United States Geological Survey as to its efficacy, especially for locating underground water, and the persistent demands that it be made a subject of investigation by the Survey. The bibliography shows that a truly astonishing number of books and pamphlets have been written on the subject. The purpose of the present brief paper is not to add another contribution to this enormous volume of uncanny literature but merely to furnish a reply to the numerous inquiries that are continually being received from all parts of the country. The outline of the history of the subject presented in the following pages will probably enable most honest inquirers to appreciate the practical uselessness of "water witching" and other applications of the divining rod, but those who wish to delve further into the mysteries of the subject are referred to the literature cited in the bibliography, in which they will find reports in painful detail of exhaustive investigations and pseudo-investigations of every phase of the subject and every imaginable explanation of the supposed phenomena.

It is doubtful whether so much investigation and discussion have been bestowed on any other subject with such absolute lack of positive results. It is difficult to see how for practical purposes the entire matter could be more thoroughly discredited, and it should be obvious to everyone that further tests by the United States Geological Survey of this so-called "witching" for water, oil, or other minerals would be a misuse of public funds.

A large number of more complicated devices for locating water or other minerals are closely related to the forked twig. A favorite trick for appealing to uneducated persons and yet making specific disproof impossible is to give as the working principle of such a device some newly discovered and vaguely understood phenomenon, as, for example, radioactivity. Many such devices have been in existence

5

since the seventeenth century, and almost without exception the claims that are made for them are very great. If any genuine instrument were invented its merits would no doubt in time become well recognized, as have those of other real inventions. The magnetic needle used in detecting iron ore is, of course, not included in this category of spurious instruments.

It is by no means true that all persons using a forked twig or some other device for locating water or other mineral are intentional deceivers. Some of them are doubtless men of good character and benevolent intentions. However, as anything that can be deeply veiled in mystery affords a good opportunity for swindlers, there can be no reasonable doubt that many of the large group of professional finders of water, oil, or other minerals who take pay for their "services" or for the sale of their "instruments" are deliberately defrauding the people, and that the total amount of money they obtain is large.

To all inquirers the United States Geological Survey therefore gives the advice not to expend any money for the services of any "water witch" or for the use or purchase of any machine or instrument devised for locating underground water or other minerals.

THE DIVINING ROD: A HISTORY OF WATER WITCHING.

By Arthur J. Ellis.

FORM OF THE DIVINING ROD.

.In its most familiar form the so-called divining rod is a forked twig, one fork of which is usually held in each hand in such a manner that the butt end of the twig normally points upward (figs. 1 and 2). The supposition is that when carried to a place beneath which water or other minerals lie, the butt end will be attracted downward, or, according to some diviners, will whirl round and round. There are many modifications in both the form and the manipulation of the device. For instance, a straight twig may be held at the small end, allowing the butt end to bob up and

FIGURE 1.—Ordinary divining rod held in the usual manner.

down, the number of bobs being taken to indicate the depth to water or ore in fathoms or feet or other common unit of measure.

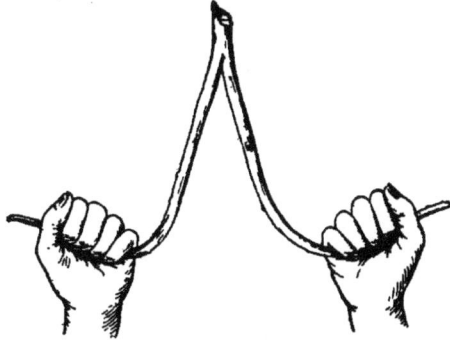

The opinion as to the kind of wood of which the twig should consist has differed greatly at different times and places, but peach, willow, hazel, and witch hazel are common favorites. By some diviners the twig is cut indiscriminately from any kind of tree, or the device is made of metal or is some common implement, such as a buggy whip. Formerly incantations were used in connection with the divining rod.

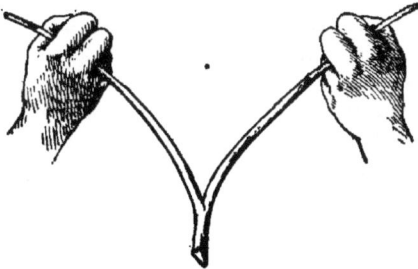

FIGURE 2.—Less common manner of holding the divining rod.

Some diviners appear to pass into abnormal or psychical states and have muscular spasms, such as occur in cases of hysteria, which, it is contended, can not be repeated at will by the

7

diviner when he returns to a normal state. Under such conditions the twig may not only rotate, but one fork may be completely twisted off by the force with which it is driven round and round.

Divining rods have been put to a wide variety of uses since the superstition first became popular, and it is not uncommon even at the present time to find them used by a single person to obtain diverse results, among which there is no conceivable relation. For example, Henri Mager purports to use the rod to detect the presence of water and ores and to measure their depth below the surface, to analyze water and ores, to determine the directions of the cardinal points, to measure the height of trees, and to perform other marvels. (See p. 23.) In tracing the history of the subject it is found that divining rods have been used for all of the following purposes: (1) To locate ore deposits, (2) to discover buried or hidden treasure, (3) to find lost landmarks and reestablish property boundaries, (4) to detect criminals, (5) to analyze personal character, (6) to cure diseases, (7) to trace lost or strayed domestic animals, (8) to insure immunity against ill fortune when preserved as a fetish, (9) to locate well sites, (10) to trace the courses of underground streams, (11) to determine the amount of water available by drilling at a given spot, (12) to determine the depth at which water or ores occur, (13) to determine the direction of cardinal points, (14) to determine the heights of trees, and (15) to analyze ores and waters.

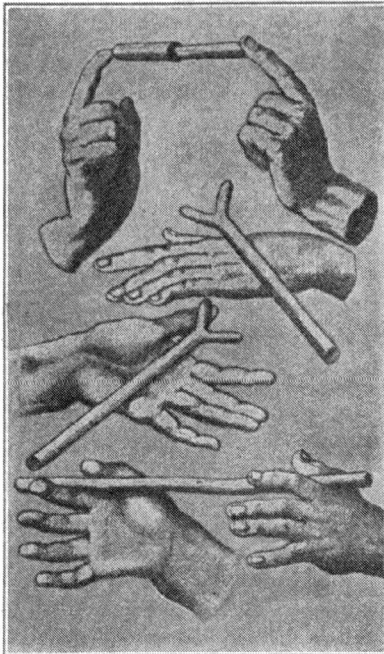

FIGURE 3.—Various old types of divining rods and the ways in which they were held. (After Valle-mont, 1693.)

ORIGIN OF THE DIVINING ROD.

The origin of the divining rod is lost in antiquity. Students of the subject have discovered in ancient literature many more or less vague references to it, and though it is certain that rods or wands of some kind were in use among ancient peoples for forecasting events and searching for lost objects, and in occult practices generally, little is known of the manner in which such rods were used or what relation, if any, they may have to the modern device. The "rod" is mentioned many times in the Bible in connection with miraculous performances, especially in the books of Moses. The much-quoted passage describing the "smiting of the rock" (Numbers xx, 9–11) has been regarded by enthusiasts of water witching as a significant reference to the divining rod,[1] as have also the following passages: "My people ask council at their stocks, and their staff declareth unto them" (Hosea iv, 12); and "The king of Babylon stood at the parting of the way, at the head of two ways, to use divination; he made his arrows bright," etc. (Ezekiel xxi, 21).

The following paragraphs are quoted from Rossiter Raymond's essay [2] on the use of rods for divination:

> The Scythians, Persians, and Medes used them. Herodotus says that the Scythians detected perjurers by means of rods. The word rhabdomancy,[3] originated by the Greeks, shows that they practiced this art; and the magic power of the rods of Minerva, Circe, and Hermes or Mercury is familiar to classical students. The lituus of the Romans, with which the augurs divined, was apparently an arched rod. Cicero, who had himself been an augur, says, in his treatise on divination, that he does not see how two augurs, meeting in the street, could look each other in the face without laughing. At the end of the first book of this treatise he quotes a couplet from the old Latin poet Ennius, representing a person from whom a diviner had demanded a fee as replying to this demand, "I will pay you out of the treasures which you enable me to find." * * *

> Marco Polo reports the use of rods or arrows for divination throughout the Orient, and a later traveler describes it among the Turks. Tacitus says that the ancient Germans used for this purpose branches of fruit trees. One of their tribes, the Frisians, employed rods in church to detect murderers. Finally, if we may trust Gonzalez de Mendoza, the Chinese, who seem to have had everything before anybody else, used pieces of wood for divination.

> Thus we perceive that the application of the divining rod in historical antiquity was mainly or wholly moral—that is, it was employed to detect guilt, decide future events, advise courses of action, etc. There are but two passages which have been quoted to prove its use for physical purposes; one from Ctesias (Apud phot. bibl. cod.), who speaks of a rod of the wood Parebus, which attracted gold, silver, other metals, stones, and several other things; the other from Cicero (De Officiis, lib. I), who says, "If we could obtain with the so-called divine rod everything pertaining to food and clothing (ad victum cultumque)," etc.[4]

> On the other hand, the silence of many authors is significant, as Chevreul has pointed out. Varro does not mention the use of the rod for the discovery of subterranean waters or metals. Vitruvius, discussing the means of discovering springs, says nothing of it. Pliny, in Book XXX of his Natural History, omits it from his enumeration of magical arts and methods, and in Book XXXI, describing (after Vitruvius) the means of discovering springs, and Book XXXIII, describing explorations for metals, is equally silent concerning it. Columella, Palladius, and in the sixth century Cassio-

---

[1] Latimer, Charles, The divining rod, p. 20, 1876.

[2] Raymond, R. W., The divining rod: Am. Inst. Min. Eng. Trans., vol. 11, pp. 415–416, 1883. See also U. S. Geol. Survey Mineral Resources, 1882, pp. 610–626, 1883.

[3] Rhabdomancy, from the Greek ῥάβδος, rod, and μαντεία, divination, is the practice of searching for springs, well sites, precious metals, and other things concealed in the earth by means of a divining rod.

[4] This reference in complete form reads as follows: "If all that is needful for our nourishment and support arrives to us by means of some divine rod, as people say, then each of us, free from all care and trouble, may give himself up to the exclusive pursuit of study and science."

dorus are likewise dumb, though the latter in one of his epistles (Theodoric, LIII) extols the utility of the professional water discoverers.

Whatever significance one may attach to such references as those cited above, no conclusive evidence has been found of the use of the divining rod as it is now known earlier than the first half of the sixteenth century. What is believed to be the first published description of the rod is contained in Georgius Agricola's "De re metallica," which was begun about 1533 and was published in 1556. There is a striking similarity between some of the ideas expressed in this account and some of those now held regarding the rod and its use, which, it is believed, justify its quotation. The following paragraphs are quoted from the Hoover translation: [1]

There are many great contentions between miners concerning the forked twig, for some say that it is of the greatest use in discovering veins, and others deny it. Some of those who manipulate and use the twig first cut a fork from a hazel bush with a knife, for this bush they consider more efficacious than any other for revealing veins, especially if the hazel bush grows above a vein. Others use a different kind of twig for each metal, when they are seeking to discover the veins, for they employ hazel twigs for veins of silver; ash twigs for copper; pitch pine for lead and especially tin, and rods made of iron and steel for gold. All alike grasp the forks of the twig with their hands, clenching their fists, it being necessary that the clenched fingers should be held toward the sky in order that the twig should be raised at that end where the two branches meet. Then they wander hither and thither at random through mountainous regions. It is said that the moment they place their feet on a vein the twig immediately turns and twists, and so by its action discloses the vein; when they move their feet again and go away from that spot the twig becomes once more immobile. The truth is, they assert, the movement of the twig is caused by the power of the veins, and sometimes this is so great that the branches of trees growing near a vein are deflected toward it. On the other hand, those who say that the twig is of no use to good and serious men, also deny that the motion is due to the power of the veins, because the twig will not move for everybody, but only for those who employ incantations and craft. Moreover, they deny the power of a vein to draw to itself the branches of trees, but they say that the warm and dry exhalations cause these contortions. Those who advocate the use of the twig make this reply to these objections: When one of the miners or some other person holds the twig in his hands, and it is not turned by the force of the veins, this is due to some peculiarity of the individual, which hinders and impedes the power of the vein, for since the power of the vein in turning and twisting the twig may be not unlike that of a magnet attracting and drawing iron toward itself, this hidden quality of a man weakens and breaks the force, just the same as garlic weakens and overcomes the strength of a magnet. For a magnet smeared with garlic juice can not attract iron, nor does it attract the latter when rusty. Further, concerning the handling of the twig, they warn us that we should not press the fingers together too lightly, nor clench them too firmly, for if the twig is held lightly they say that it will fall before the force of the vein can turn it; if, however, it is grasped too firmly the force of the hands resists the force of the veins and counteracts it. Therefore, they consider that five things are necessary to insure that the twig shall serve its purpose: of these the first is the size of the twig, for the force of the vein can not turn too large a stick; secondly, there is the shape of the twig, which must be forked or the vein can not turn it; thirdly, the power of the vein which has the nature to turn it; fourthly, the manipulation of the twig; fifthly, the absence of

----

[1] Agricola, Georgius, De re metallica, translated from first Latin edition of 1556 by H. C. and L. H. Hoover, pp. 38–41, 1912.

impeding peculiarities. These advocates of the twig sum up their conclusions as follows: If the rod does not move for everybody, it is due to unskilled manipulation or to the impeding peculiarities of the man which oppose and resist the force of the veins, as we said above, and those who search for veins by means of the twig need not necessarily make incantations, but it is sufficient that they handle it suitably and are devoid of impeding power; therefore, the twig may be of use to good and serious men in discovering veins. With regard to deflection of branches of trees they say nothing and adhere to their opinion.

Since this matter remains in dispute and causes much dissension amongst miners, I consider it ought to be examined on its own merits. The wizards, who also make use of rings, mirrors, and crystals, seek for veins with a divining rod shaped like a fork; but its shape makes no difference in the matter—it might be straight or of some other form—for it is not the form of the twig that matters [see fig. 3], but the wizard's incantations which it would not become me to repeat, neither do I wish to do so. The ancients, by means of the divining rod, not only procured those things necessary for a livelihood or for luxury, but they were able also to alter the forms of things by it; as when the magicians changed the rods of the Egyptians into serpents, as the writings of the Hebrews relate; and as in Homer, Minerva with a divining rod turned the aged Ulysses suddenly into a youth and then restored him back again to old age; Circe also changed Ulysses' companions into beasts, but afterward gave them back again their human forms; moreover, by his rod, which was called "Caduceus," Mercury gave sleep to watchmen and awoke slumberers. Therefore it seems that the divining rod passed to the mines from its impure origin with the magicians. Then when good men shrank with horror from incantations and rejected them, the twig was retained by the unsophisticated common miners, and in searching for new veins some traces of these ancient usages remain.

But since truly the twigs of the miners do move, albeit they do not generally use incantations, some say this movement is caused by the power of the veins, others say that it depends on the manipulation, and still others think that the movement is due to both these causes. But, in truth, all those objects which are endowed with the power of attraction do not twist things in circles, but attract them directly to themselves; for instance, the magnet does not turn the iron but draws it directly to itself, and amber rubbed until it is warm does not bend straws about, but simply draws them to itself. If the power of the veins were of a similar nature to that of the magnet and the amber, the twig would not so much twist as move once only, in a semicircle, and be drawn directly to the vein, and unless the strength of the man who holds the twig were to resist and oppose the force of the vein the twig would be brought to the ground; wherefore, since this is not the case, it must necessarily follow that the manipulation is the cause of the twig's twisting motion. It is a conspicuous fact that these cunning manipulators do not use a straight twig but a forked one cut from a hazel bush or from some other wood equally flexible, so that if it be held in the hands, as they are accustomed to hold it, it turns in a circle for any man wherever he stands. Nor is it strange that the twig does not turn when held by the inexperienced, because they either grasp the forks of the twig too tightly or hold them too loosely. Nevertheless, these things give rise to the faith among common miners that veins are discovered by the use of twigs, because whilst using these they do accidentally discover some; but it more often happens that they lose their labour, and although they might discover a vein, they become none the less exhausted in digging useless trenches than do the miners who prospect in an unfortunate locality. Therefore a miner, since we think he ought to be a good and serious man, should not make use of an enchanted twig, because if he is prudent and skilled in the natural signs he understands that a forked stick is of no use to him, for, as I have said before, there are the natural indications of the veins which he can see for himself without the help of twigs. So if Nature or chance should indicate a locality suitable for mining, the miner should dig his trenches there; if no vein appears he must dig numerous trenches until he discovers an outcrop of a vein.

There are two accounts of earlier date than "De re metallica" which are mentioned in most histories of the divining rod. One of these accounts is contained in the "Novum testamentum" of Basilius Valentinus, a Benedictine monk of the fifteenth century, who devoted seven chapters of the second book of his work to a didactic account of the use of the divining rod. But there is some confusion as to the date and as to the authorship of this book, and Raymond points out that the existence even of Basilius Valentinus is not beyond doubt. Gadenus states, in his "Historia Erfordiensis" (1675), that Basilius was living at St. Peter's convent at Erfurth in 1413, but the earliest copy of the "Testamentum," which is a French translation in manuscript, is dated 1651, and the book was not printed until about fifty years after Agricola. The other account is contained in "De natura rerum," IX, by Paracelsus, which was no doubt written prior to "De re metallica," for Paracelsus died in 1541, but it was not published until some time later. From this account Hoover [1] quotes:

These [divinations] are vain and misleading, and among the first of them are divining rods, which have deceived many miners. If they once point rightly they deceive ten or twenty times.

Barrett [2] considers it practically certain that the birthplace of the modern divining rod is in the mining districts of Germany, probably in the Harz Mountains, where the most approved mining processes were first devised. He says:

Possibly they were led to its use from the belief, once universal among educated men like Melanchthon, that metallic ores attracted certain trees which thereupon drooped over the place where those ores were to be found, the drooping no doubt being due to the soil or other causes. A branch of the tree was therefore cut and held to see where it drooped; later on a branch was held in each hand and the extremities tied together, as shown in an old Italian plate [See fig. 4]; finally, for convenience, a forked branch was cut, the two ends grasped one in each hand with palms upward; the arms of the holder were then brought to the side of the body, so that the forked rod was held in somewhat unstable equilibrium, and the "diviner" set forth on his quest with, in old time, certain solemnities and invocations.

At any rate the divining rod came into common use first in Germany as a means for locating mines and also for discovering buried treasure, a matter of rather common interest in those days, when the practice of burying money and plate for safe keeping was so general.

SPREAD OF THE DELUSION.

German miners were imported into England during the reign of Elizabeth (1558–1603) to lend an impetus to the industry in Cornwall, which had been passing through a period of depression. By them the divining rod was introduced into England, and before the end of the seventeenth century it had spread through the countries of Europe. Everywhere it aroused controversy. Its champions, among

1 Hoover, H. C. and L. H., Agricola, De re metallica, p. 38, 1912.
2 Barrett, W. F., Soc. Psych. Res. Proc., vol. 13, p. 13, 1897–98.

whom were some of the most learned men of the time, explained its operation, as, indeed, they explained nearly all facts of physics and chemistry, on the principle of "sympathy" or "attraction and repulsion." The common phenomena of gravity and magnetism doubtless suggested this interpretation. Philippe Melanchthon, in his "Discours sur la sympathie," 15—?; his son-in-law, Gaspar Peucer, in "Les devins," 1584 (book 13, ch. 10); Porta, in "Magiae naturalis,"

FIGURE 4.—Use of divining rods in prospecting for ore. A, Twig; B, trench. (From Agricola, De re metallica, German edition, 1580.)

1569(book 1, ch. 8); Keckermann(1573-1609)in "Systemata physica" (book 1, ch. 8); and Michel Mayer, in "Verum inventum," 1619 (ch. 4), attribute the action of the divining rod to "sympathetic affinity."

The adversaries of the divining rod, on the other hand, like Paracelsus and Agricola, condemned its use as a superstitious and vain practice, without attempting to refute the specific arguments advanced by their opponents or flatly denying its supernatural connections.

A third view was that involving a demoniac influence, and Raymond suggests that the adversaries of the rod, including Agricola, may have adopted their attitude of reserve on the question of Satanic influences from a desire to avoid possible serious consequences. Another view, closely related to that of satanic influence, is described by Raymond [1] as follows:

A fourth view was indeed advanced, according to which the operator, as well as the rod, was the recipient of a divinely given faculty. It was no doubt with the purpose of avoiding the odium attached to dealings with the Evil One that the professors of this science, particularly in Germany, surrounded it with ceremonies and formulas of a highly pious character. It is true that the rules sometimes prescribed for the cutting of the twig partook largely of heathen sorcery and astrology. They were indeed, to some extent, unconscious reminiscences of the old Scandinavian, and even of the Aryan mythology. But this was atoned for when the rod was duly Christianized by baptism, being laid for this purpose in the bed with a newly baptized child, by whose Christian name it was afterward addressed. The following formula, cited by Gaetzschmann, may serve as an example: "In the name of the Father and of the Son and of the Holy Ghost, I adjure thee, Augusta Carolina, that thou tell me, so pure and true as Mary the Virgin was, who bore our Lord Jesus Christ, how many fathoms is it from here to the ore?" In this case, the rod was expected to reply by dipping a certain number of times, corresponding to the number of fathoms,

It is readily conceivable that the motive for surrounding this practice with a religious atmosphere might not have been altogether a belief in its divine character, for at that time anyone found engaged in mysterious works was in danger of being charged with sorcery and burned to death.

In Cornwall the belief was common among the miners and still persists as a tradition, that the divining rod was guided to the ore deposits by the pixies, the fairy custodians of the mineral treasures of the earth.

Not only did the abstract discussion of this subject engage the attention of persons in all classes of society, but nobles and peasants, priests and philosophers—representatives from every class—busied themselves trying to locate ore deposits by means of forked twigs. Probably the most prominent diviners at this time were Baron de Beausoleil (Jean-Jacques de Chatelet), 1576–1643, and his wife. Beausoleil, who was one of the foremost mining authorities of his day, traveled extensively through the mining regions of Europe, visited America in his study of mining, and received important commissions from dukes and emperors, and even from the Pope. His wife shared his responsibilities and honors. But later they fell from favor through the machinations of rivals, and the fact that they used divining rods and other contrivances was made the basis of a charge of sorcery. After some years of persecution they were placed in prison (1642), the baron in the Bastile and his wife in Vincennes, where they died about 1645. Raymond [2] writes:

In magnifying the art of discovering mines and springs, and the skill required for this purpose, she [the baroness, in "The restitution of Pluto"] gives a description of

[1] Raymond, R. W., The divining rod: Am. Inst. Min. Eng. Trans., vol. 11, p. 419, 1883.
[2] Idem, pp. 420–421.

the means employed, showing that these hidden treasures are to be detected, (1) by digging, which is the least important way, (2) by the herbs and plants which grow above streams of water, (3) by the taste of the waters which flow from them, (4) by the vapors which arise from them at sunrise, and (5) by the use of 16 scientific instruments and 7 rods [the 7 rods of Basilius Valentinus] connected with the 7 planets," etc.

The first four means were undoubtedly real and really employed. Under the fifth head we have an illustration of what is so common in the alchemistic and other medieval writers, namely, the covering of the facts of nature and the methods of investigation with assumed mystery to hide them from the vulgar.

⁻ This raises the interesting question as to the extent to which intelligent persons may have used divining rods in the early days for the sole purpose of concealing from the uninitiated their real methods of prospecting. One can hardly overestimate the respect for the divining rod that would be created among common miners if a man of real ability publicly attributed his success to its use, and it may be that the deep-rooted hold which the superstition obtained on the popular mind was due to just such circumstances as this.

ORIGIN OF "WATER WITCHING."

The above quotation from the Baroness Beausoleil is interesting also for the reason that in it the divining rod is mentioned as a means of discovering springs. The Beausoleils are believed to have been influential in bringing about the use of forked twigs in searching for water, although Barrett [1] writes as follows in regard to an account which he finds in a Life of Saint Teresa of Spain:

Teresa in 1568 was offered the site for a convent to which there was only one objection—there was no water supply; happily, a Friar Antonio came up with a twig in his hand, stopped at a certain spot, and appeared to be making the sign of the cross; but Teresa says, "Really I can not be sure if it were the sign he made, at any rate he made some movement with the twig and then he said, ' Dig just here'; they dug, and lo! a plentiful fount of water gushed forth, excellent for drinking, copious for washing, and it never ran dry."

Barrett regards this the first historical reference to "dowsing" for water, but Mager [2] and Klinckowstroem [3] mention a paper written by Claude Galien in 1630 on the supposed discovery of the Chateau-Thierry mineral water by Baroness Beausoleil as the first reference. At any rate, from about this time on the divining rod was used in southern Europe as much in the search for water as in the search for mines, although, according to Barrett, it was not used for this purpose in England until near the end of the eighteenth century.

This new application of the divining rod no doubt tended to popularize it. It had been of interest chiefly to miners, and outside of mining districts it was probably known only in a vague sort of way. But as a "water finder" it became more generally known,

[1] Barrett, W. F., Psychical research, p. 171, 1911.
[2] Mager, Henri, Les moyens de découvrir les eaux souterraines et de les utiliser, p. 327, 1912.
[3] Klinckowstroem, Graf Carl v., Bibliographie der Wünschelrute, p. 38, 1911.

and in the very nature of things its successes must have outnumbered its failures, just as, taking the country over, successful wells outnumber unsuccessful ones.

ECCLESIASTICAL CONTROVERSIES.

The divining rod continued to be a favorite subject with alchemistic writers until about 1660, when a new turn of affairs was brought about largely by the Jesuit Father Gaspard Schott, who, in his "Magiae universalis naturae et artis" (1659), denounced it as an instrument controlled by the devil. The subject was then taken up by the church, and for more than 100 years it was hotly debated by churchmen. Some approved of the rod and authorized its use on church property; others condemned it and threatened those who used it with excommunication. Gaspard Schott later expressed the belief that its movements were probably not caused by the devil, as "monks of great piety have used it with really marvelous success, and affirm positively that the movement is entirely natural and that it does not at all proceed from dexterity or from the strength of imagination of him who uses it," and he and A. Kircher were the first to advance the theory that the movement of the rod is due to unconscious muscular action.

About 1671 Matthaeus Willenius published an account of the mercury wand, in which he stoutly defended the use of the divining rod, and two years later Jacques Le Royer announced that the material of which the rod is made is of little consequence, as he claimed to have obtained equally good results with rods made of wood, oxhorn, ivory, gold, or silver.

In 1674 the Jesuit priest Dechales wrote (in "De fontibus naturalibus"):

There are two things which astonish me in this experience: Why this rod turns only in the hands of certain persons, and second, why this rod serves equally well to locate both underground streams and mines.

In 1675 J. C. Frommann, a doctor of medicine, ridiculed those who explained the movements of the rod as a sleight-of-hand trick, and compared the mystery of the rod with the mystery of reproduction. In 1684 another doctor of medicine (G. B. de Saint-Romain) explained the movements of the rod as due to emanations given off from minerals and underground streams.

USE OF THE DIVINING ROD IN DETECTING CRIMINALS.

Prior to 1692 the divining rod had been used in trying to locate minerals and water and possibly to some extent for other purposes. But in that year an incident occurred in southern France which added greatly to the notoriety of the divining rod and extended its field of operation into the moral world, in which, according to some writers (p. 9), rods for divination had their origin. This incident, which is described in great detail by several writers,[1] was the apprehension and identification of a criminal through the agency of a peasant of Dauphiny named Jacques Aymar, who claimed the ability to trace fugitives by the use of divining rods.

Interest in this case was intense and widespread and called forth a large amount of literature. In commenting on the case Barrett[2] says:

> The other one, a hunchback, who was arrested, confessed the crime and was executed: the last person in Europe who suffered that terrible penalty of being "broken at the wheel." * * * Strangely enough the depositions made at the trial showed that Aymar was correct in every detail, witnesses testifying to the flight and halting places of the culprits in the very places Aymar had indicated. * * * Aymar became notorious throughout Europe. He was, however, subsequently somewhat discredited owing to his failure in some tests devised by the Prince de Condé.

But Raymond, in a decidedly more skeptical treatment of the matter, raises some illuminating questions in regard to Aymar's integrity. His comment on the work of Aymar[3] includes the following statements:

> This man, Jacques Aymar by name, was sent for—or rather it was not necessary to send for him, since he proved to be already on hand in the city by the time it was decided to engage his services. This fact is significant as giving the key to what turned out to be an extraordinary piece of clever detective work. A careful analysis of the numerous official and other records of this case shows it to be quite possible that the diviner had obtained important clues before he was publicly set to work. * * * The subsequent tracking of a hunchback would be no very difficult matter. * * * But this achievement of the rod, attested as it was by official records and by the public confession and execution of the criminal made a great sensation in France. * * * Aymar was called to Paris, where both the court and the savants interested themselves greatly in his mysterious powers. Many marvelous feats are reported of him there; but the shrewd and rigorous experiments of the Prince de Condé exposed the emptiness of his pretensions * * *. As late as 1703 this man was employed during the civil war to point out with his divining rod Protestants for massacre, under the plea of punishment for crimes they had committed.

The belief that the divining rod was an instrument invented by Satan for the confusion of men was no doubt as old as the superstition itself, but, as previously indicated, it was greatly strengthened when in 1659 Gaspard Schott proclaimed that the rod was controlled by the devil, thereby identifying it with witchcraft and bringing it within the jurisdiction of the Church. Although the use of the divining rod differed essentially from witchcraft in many respects, nevertheless, in addition to its direct implication by its ecclesiastical adversaries, there was in some respects a very close relation between the two, as

---

[1] Baring-Gould, Sabine, Curious myths of the middle ages, p. 54, 1894. Mager, Henri, Les moyens de découvrir les eaux souterraines et de les utiliser, pp. 362-365, 1912.

[2] Psychical research, ch. 12, p. 172.

[3] Raymond, R. W., The divining rod: Am. Soc. Min. Eng. Trans., vol. 11, pp. 424-427, 1883.

is suggested by the use of incantations in connection with divining, and to this relationship may be ascribed in some measure the strengthening of belief in the rod. The significance of this lies in the fact that witchcraft, at the time of the Aymar episode, had become a frenzy, and anything—even the simplest occurrences of everyday life—which by any stretch of the imagination could be suspected of implication with witchcraft, became a subject of discussion and the basis of firm opinions and beliefs.

In view of the prevalence of such beliefs as this reign of delusion implies, it is by no means difficult to account for the credence accorded to such claims as those made by Jacques Aymar. Moreover, considering the ordeals of torture inflicted on persons accused of crime to extract confessions, by a strange perversion called "voluntary," and often inflicted on the witnesses as well, and considering also the fact that a public execution was sometimes regarded as a highly diverting spectacle well worth some effort to bring it about, the testimony supporting the claims of Aymar, as repeated to us, combined even with the reported confession of the accused, falls far short of establishing the merit claimed by Aymar, or even the guilt of the hunchback who was executed.

In 1701 the Inquisition issued a decree against the further use of the divining rod in criminal prosecution, and this use of the device rapidly came to an end.

SCIENTIFIC CONTROVERSIES.

LEBRUN AND OTHERS.

For about 80 years after the decree by the Inquisition abolishing its use for the detection of criminals the divining rod continued to be a fruitful subject for debate among ecclesiastical authorities, among whom was Pierre Lebrun, who in 1692 first suggested the theory of "prior intention," but in 1780 it was dropped and received no further official recognition by churchmen. But the time was then ripe for controversies along an altogether new line, namely, the attempt to explain water witching as an electrical phenomenon. About this time the study of electricity was making great progress, especially through the work of Volta and Galvani, and the demonstration by Galvani that amputated legs of frogs could be made to twitch under the influence of electrical stimuli was at once misinterpreted by advocates of the divining rod as giving a scientific basis for water witching.

THOUVENEL.

The controversies relating to electrical phenomena were begun by Pierre Thouvenel, a physician to Louis XVI, who interested himself in another peasant of Dauphiny, Barthélemy Bleton, who, like Jacques Aymar, had acquired notoriety as a "hydroscope."

Bleton was born at Bouvantes, in Dauphiny, in 1750, or possibly a few years earlier, was brought up by charity in a monastery, and became a herdsman. The first manifestation of "hydroscopic" faculties in Bleton is described in the following paragraph quoted from Barrett,[1] who gives it as a translation from Thouvenel's correspondence dated at Dijon, April 14, 1781:

> Bleton when 7 years of age had carried dinner to some workmen; he sat down on a stone, when a fever or faintness seized him; the workmen having brought him to their side, the faintness ceased; but each time he returned to the stone he suffered again. This was told to the Prior of the Chartreuse, who wished to see it for himself. Being thus convinced of the. fact, he had the ground under the stone dug up; there they found a spring, which, I am told, is still in use to turn a mill.

Thouvenel heard of Bleton and chose him as a fit subject on whom to test his notions of "animal magnetism," and as a result published an elaborate essay which he called "Mémoire physique et médicinal, montrant des rapports évidents entre les phénomènes de la baguette divinatoire, du magnétisme et de l'électricité." The following account by Raymond[2] presents the principal facts in regard to Bleton's achievements in concise form:

> In the first place, Bleton apparently did not profess to discover immaterial qualities or facts, but chiefly confined himself to the detection of running water. In the second place, he frankly avowed that the rod possessed no power in itself by virtue of its form or material, and that it was merely an index, outwardly exhibiting to the spectators his inward feeling. This feeling the doctor declared to be a tremor, attacking first the diaphragm and communicating itself through the body and. hands to the rod. In the third place this tremor was found by Dr. Thouvenel to be weakened, though not destroyed, when Bleton was on a tree or ladder or another person's shoulder, instead of the ground, or when he touched electrified substances; but the tremor and also the movement of the rod were completely stopped when Bleton was insulated from the ground. Upon facts of this kind he based his electrical theory. I remark, by the way, that the observations and the theory of Mr. Latimer, in his recent work on the divining rod, already mentioned, recall in a striking manner the performances of Bleton and the theory of Thouvenel. Mr. Latimer claims to have made the new discovery that the effect of the divining rod is destroyed by insulating the practitioner, as, for instance, by placing him upon a platform supported by glass bottles. If he had known how thoroughly this claim had been examined and refuted, almost exactly 100 years ago, he would have had less faith in its novelty and value.

Thouvenel's book made no little sensation, and in 1782 Bleton was called to Paris, where a remarkable series of experimental tests were applied to him. A newspaper report of the day declares that in the presence of many thousands of spectators he followed a subterranean aqueduct in the garden of the Luxembourg for 15,000 yards without a mistake. The chief engineer of the waterworks is reported to have said that the trace was so accurate that if the maps of his office had been lost, Bleton's footsteps would have constituted a complete survey to replace them. It is just possible that the Journal de Paris was tempted to make a sensation of this case, and it is also quite possible that a keen observer might notice indications other than those of his own diaphragm, by which he could follow the line of buried pipes. A large number of experiments, more calmly reported, certainly do not sustain the

[1] Barrett, W. F., On the so-called divining rod: Soc. Psych. Res. Proc., vol. 15, p. 257, 1900.
[2] Raymond, R. W., The divining rod: Am. Inst. Min. Eng. Trans., vol. 11, pp. 431–433, 1883.

enthusiasm of this account. It was found, for instance, that Bleton often passed over running water, when blindfolded, without noticing it; and that when taken several times over the same course he would not point out accurately each time the spots which he had previously marked. For example, of 16 points once indicated, he recognized with the rod on the second round but eight and missed the other eight. A single point to which he was repeatedly brought blindfold he indicated three times and missed three times. Of seven channels of running water which he was made to cross repeatedly, he indicated one once in four times, another once in four times, and another once in three times, while still another, which he crossed in two spots, affected his diaphragm at one crossing and not at all at the other. The insulation experiment was repeated by a physician at Paris. At a point where Bleton's rod was powerfully affected by alleged subterranean water, he was mounted upon a stool with glass legs, and immediately the rod ceased to be affected. When the stool was removed, however, and he stood upon the ground, the rod resumed its sensitiveness. But Dr. Charles, who conducted this experiment, took occasion, while Bleton stood upon the stool, to bring the top, without his knowledge, into electrical communication with the earth by means of a good conductor, thus destroying the insulation completely, though the hydroscopist supposed it still to exist. Under these circumstances the rod remained inactive, and the destruction of insulation did not produce the slightest result. This was declared at the time to be a proof of Bleton's charlatanry; but, as we shall see hereafter, it is equally consistent with the hypothesis of unconscious mental and muscular action.

As a final test of Bleton's capacity as a hydroscopist, he was taken blindfold into the new church of Saint Genevieve, where there was known to be no water for 100 feet below the floor, the vaults, foundations, etc., actually extending all that distance below. Here he professed to discover at numerous points large and small streams of water. Thouvenel subsequently asserted that his protégé had been affected by currents of damp air circulating in the cellar, but this explanation was universally considered as a desperate attempt to maintain a theory already brought into discredit by experimental tests. Bleton, however, though he ceased to be seriously respected by impartial scientists, continued to receive much attention, and to do a thriving business, both in Paris and subsequently in the provinces. Here, however, he no longer worked blindfold or professed to see with his diaphragm. He proceeded like the ordinary water diviners, with open eyes, studying all the natural indications, and coming to his decisions with abundant leisure; and under the circumstances it, is beyond doubt that he rendered many valuable services to landed proprietors by successfully locating wells. In many cases, however, he failed entirely, and it is reported that even in those in which he succeeded, he was seldom right as to the depth at which water would be found or the quantity which would be obtained. It should be mentioned that in Dauphiny, where Bleton discovered a large number of springs, he was regarded with an esteem never given to Aymar and some other famous hydroscopists. In other words, the people who knew most about the art of discovering water pronounced Bleton to be a real expert, while they believed Aymar and Parangue to be more or less charlatans. A review of all the facts leaves little doubt that in Bleton's case there was an unusually large proportion of the skill of the prospector, combined with rather less than usual of the mysterious claims of the wizard.

At this time many diviners acquired notoriety, including Parangue and Pennet, of Dauphiny, and Campetti, of Italy, but their careers differed in no significant respect from that of Bleton. The feature of this time was the patronage of diviners by scientists and the attempt to apply hypotheses of animal magnetism and terrestrial electricity to the supposed operation of the divining rod.

CHEVREUL AND FARADAY.

During the first half of the nineteenth century the phenomena of "table turning" was introduced, and became so popular that it was often employed in drawing-room entertainments. During this time also the so-called "magic pendulum," which had persisted from antiquity as a rather obscure divining instrument, was popularized and an elaborate system of electrical hypotheses was based on its conduct. The magic pendulum consists of a finger ring, watch, piece of metal, or any other suitable weight, attached to the end of a cord and suspended from the hand. In ancient times it was used to forecast events by suspending it over a disk on the margin of which were the letters of the alphabet, the pendulum being brought to rest and held steadily until it finally began to swing, thereby pointing out various letters which formed or suggested the words of a prophecy. It is said to be fairly common as a toy at the present time and is still occasionally used seriously by superstitious people in this country. At the beginning of the eighteenth century it was being used, like the divining rod, in attempts to locate well sites, for which purpose it is still used to some extent. In 1812, however, Michel Eugene Chevreul made an investigation of the subject and concluded that the whole phenomenon was a result of involuntary muscular movements in the hand, induced by mental processes.

In 1854 Michael Faraday showed that table turning was due to involuntary muscular movements; and in the same year Chevreul, as a member of a committee appointed by the Academy of Science to investigate the divining rod and the magic pendulum, wrote with regard to the divining rod:

It is evident to my eyes that the cause of the movement of the wand does not belong to the physical world, but to the moral world; I think that, in most of the cases in hand, in which the wand is held by an honest man who has faith in it, the movement is the consequence of an act of the mind of that man.

The foundation of the science of psychology was being laid at this time, and psychical phenomena were just beginning to be recognized in a new light. In the conclusions of Faraday and Chevreul, therefore, may be recognized the first application of those new conceptions of mental processes. This theory was finally elaborated in an exhaustive treatment of the subject by Barrett. (See pp. 22–23.)

LATIMER.

While all these investigations were being conducted in Europe the divining rod was enjoying a peaceful existence in the United States, forked twigs being used more or less in prospecting for water, oil, and other mineral deposits. But in 1875 Charles Latimer[1] read before

---

[1] Latimer, Charles, The divining rod: virgula divina baculus divinatoribus, water witching, Cleveland, 1876.

the Civil Engineers' Club of the Northwest an essay on "The divining rod," which was later published (1876) with additional notes, in which he undertook to prove that the operation of the rod depends on electrical currents transmitted from the ground through the body, inducing a magnetic field between the rod and the ground. He also explained a method by which he claimed to be able to determine the amount of water available and the depth at which it would be reached.

RAYMOND.

In 1883 R. W. Raymond [1] published his essay on "The divining rod," which contains a historical outline of the subject and a set of conclusions based especially on the works of Chevreul. It concludes with the following highly rhetorical epitaph on this venerable superstition:

To this, then, the rod of Moses, of Jacob, of Mercury, of Circe, of Valentin, of Beausoleil, of Vallemont, of Aymar, of Bleton, of Pennet, of Campetti—even of Mr. Latimer—has come at last. In itself it is nothing. Its claims to virtues derived from Deity, from Satan, from affinities and sympathies, from corpuscular effluvia, from electrical currents, from passive perturbatory qualities of organo-electric force are hopelessly collapsed and discarded. A whole library of learned rubbish about it which remains to us furnishes jargon for charlatans, marvelous tales for fools, and amusement for antiquarians; otherwise it is only fit to constitute part of Mr. Caxton's "History of human error." And the sphere of the divining rod has shrunk with its authority. In one department after another it has been found useless. Even in the one application left to it with any show of reason it is nothing unless held in skillful hands, and whoever has the skill may dispense with the rod. It belongs, with "the magic pendulum" and "planchette," among the toys of children. Or, if it be worthy the attention of scientific students, it is the students of psychology and biology, not of geology and hydroscopy and the science of ore deposits, who can profitably consider it.

BARRETT.

In 1891 W. F. Barrett,[2] professor of physics in the Royal College of Science for Ireland, in the interest of the Society for Psychical Research, undertook· a very laborious investigation of water witching, or dowsing, as it is called in England, and later published his results in two large volumes.

Barrett concluded that the movement of the rod or forked twig is due to unconscious muscular action arising from subconscious and involuntary "suggestion" impressed on the mind of the dowser, and that this subconscious suggestion may be merely an autosuggestion or a suggestion derived through the senses from the environment, but that in a certain number of cases it appears to be due to a subconscious perceptive power commonly called clairvoyance. His conclu-

[1] Raymond, R. W., The divining rod: Am. Inst. Min. Eng. Trans., vol. 11, pp. 411–446, 1883. Published also in U. S. Geol. Survey Mineral Resources, 1882, pp. 610–626, 1883.

[2] Barrett, W. F., On the so-called divining rod or Virgula divina: Soc. Psych. Res., Proc., vols. 13 and 15, 1897, 1901.

sions were therefore in a sense favorable to water witching, although completely refuting all claims that there is any physical relation between the underground water and the forked twig or its manipulator, and definitely relegating the subject wholly to the obscure realm of occultism with other varieties of fortune telling.

MAGER.

In all its weird history no more extravagant and absurd claims were ever made for the divining rod than those which are maintained at the present time by Henri Mager. (See p. 8.) Mager is an enthusiastic champion of divining rods, magic pendulums, and his own mechanical device for locating water and ores. His hypotheses are presented in his three elaborate volumes—"Les moyens de découvrir les eaux souterraines et de les utiliser," 1912; "Les sourciers et leurs procédés," 1913; and "Les influences des corps minéraux," 1913—and in his pamphlet "A new method for the study of mining fields and for finding ore embedded in deep ground," 1914. At almost every step in the advance of science and philosophy some one has attempted to explain the supposed operation of the divining rod by means of the latest scientific theories, and Mager's work is in accord with precedent. His claims are built on dicta or speculations in which use is made of the terminology of students of radioactivity and electromagnetism.

RECENT INVESTIGATIONS.

It remains to be stated that there are several societies in Germany whose sole object is said to be the study of the divining rod, and that a subcommittee of the commission of scientific studies in the bureau of waters and forests of the department of agriculture of France was appointed in 1910 to investigate the subject and in 1914 was still investigating.

MECHANICAL WATER FINDERS.

About 1640 Baroness Beausoleil, in "The restitution of Pluto" (see p. 16), listed, among means of discovering mines and springs, the use of 16 "scientific instruments." This is the earliest reference to such instruments that has been discovered in the preparation of this report, and it is a matter of considerable interest that even at this early date a single prospector should manifest so wide an acquaintance with devices for finding water and ore. It is certain that Beausoleil's 16 were the forerunners of a prolific race. At least 24 patents of this nature are now on file in the United States Patent Office, but this is no index to the number which have been rejected and which have never been offered for patent in this country, not to mention foreign inventions.

---

[1] See Joly, J., Radioactivity and geology, 1909, and Bauer, L. A., The physical theory of the earth's magnetic and electrical phenomena: Terrestrial magnetism and atmospheric electricity, vols. 15 and 16, 1910, 1911.

Most of the present devices are magnetic or electrical instruments, which, taken together, cover almost every application of magnetism and electricity. They range from ordinary dip needles to telephones and devices using wireless waves. Among the most widely advertised instruments of this kind are W. Mansfield's "Patent automatic water and oil finders," Henri Mager's "Indicator of current ground water," and Adolf Schmids's "Device for detecting subterranean waters." Mansfield's instrument was denied a patent in the United States on the ground that it was anticipated by the patent of Adolf Schmids. Mager's instrument, which is described in all his publications (see p. 23), is admitted by him to be only a modification of Schmids's device.

In the letters patent[1] of the Schmids device it is stated that the apparatus will "indicate certain atmospheric changes, the nature and cause of which are not yet understood but which manifest themselves in a peculiar way in the neighborhood of the source and course of subterranean waters by rapid oscillations of the pointer of the device."

The instrument is described as a hollow glass cylinder having an axis around which is spirally wound a soft-iron wire in layers that are separated from one another by paraffined paper, and at intervals by layers of tin foil. The outside layer of the spool is covered with paper. The wire of this spool forms an open circuit. The end of the spool is covered with a glass dial plate having at its center a pivot on which a pointer or needle oscillates.

It is claimed that when the instrument is in the vicinity of a source or a stream of subterranean water the needle will after a time oscillate rapidly.

In the literature advertising its "automatic water and oil finders," circulated by the Mansfield Co., of Liverpool, England, the following claims are made:

The principle on which the instrument works is the indicating of the presence of currents which flow between earth and atmosphere, and which seeking the path of greatest conductivity, are always strongest in the vicinity of subterranean water courses, the waters of which are charged with electricity to a certain degree. In taking observations, wooden pegs are placed at intervals of 20 paces in a direction usually southeast to northwest. The instrument is tried over each of these pegs in turn, and should the needle move on any one of them, tests are made all round it, and the spot where the greatest movement of the needle is obtained is where the boring should be made. If the needle does not move subterranean water does not exist under the spot where the instrument is fixed. * * * The instrument indicates water courses flowing underground in a natural state and not water pipes or sources that have sprung up to daylight.

Systematic magnetic observations have been made for about 70 years, and a complete magnetic survey of the earth, under the direction of the Carnegie Institution of Washington, has been in progress for a number of years, but this survey has not yet disclosed the existence of local earth-air currents on which to base a method of utilizing such currents in determining underground conditions. In view of this lack of knowledge any invention based on the assumption that such currents exist, as, for example, the Schmid patent, is subject to the general criticism that it is unsound in principle, or at least that, like the divining rod, it can be subjected to no conclusive scientific test. The practical use of such instruments, moreover, seems to be incompatible with the known instability of the magnetic and electric state of the earth and the atmosphere, in which disturbances of greater or less degree are constantly taking place. Investigations[1] have shown that magnetic disturbance is nearly continuous; that an entirely undisturbed day is abnormal. Some magnetic disturbances are local; others affect the whole earth simultaneously.[2] Bauer[3] writes:

The magnetic disturbances experienced by the earth are generally of a very complicated nature and reach at times startling magnitudes. Thus during the most remarkable magnetic storm of which there is any record—the one of September 25, 1909—the compass needle in the vicinity of the city of Washington suffered a change of 5 degrees in the short space of a quarter of an hour and the force acting on it passed through a change during the same period amounting to 10 per cent of its full value. * * *

I confidently expect, as soon as a complete analysis has been made of magnetic disturbances covering the greater portion of the earth, it will be found that * * * the disturbances will themselves reveal effects from terrestrial, continental, regional, and even local causes (earth currents, for example, whose path and intensity depend upon local character of soil, etc.).[4]

Since the earth's magnetic state is known to be of a very heterogeneous character, requiring an exceedingly complicated mathematical expression for even a very approximate representation, it may be confidently expected that any magnetic change or disturbance, from whatever source it may come and of however simple a type it may originally be, by the time it has entered the earth's field and has impressed itself upon our magnetic instruments, will have been converted into an equally complex type to that of the earth's magnetism itself.[5]

Further study of this subject tends merely to strengthen the belief that magnetic disturbances may be due to causes so many and various that no confidence can reasonably be placed in any claim that the oscillations of a magnetic needle indicate the occurrence of available ground water, much less the depth at which water can be reached or the quantity that can be obtained; and it confirms the opinion that, in the present state of knowledge, any such claim is purely speculative.

---

[1] Bauer, L. A., Analysis of the magnetic disturbance of Jan. 26, 1903, and general considerations regarding magnetic changes: Terrestrial magnetism and atmospheric electricity, vol. 15, pp. 22, 24, and 25, 1910.

[2] Schuster, Arthur, The diurnal variation of terrestrial magnetism: Roy. Soc. London Philos. Trans., ser. A, vol. 208, pp. 184–185, 1908.

[3] Bauer, L. A., The physical theory of the earth's magnetic and electric phenomena: Terrestrial magnetism and atmospheric electricity, vol. 15, p. 111, 1910.

[4] Op. cit. (Analysis, etc.), p. 25.

[5] Idem, p. 22.

26   THE DIVINING ROD.

BIBLIOGRAPHY OF "WATER WITCHING."

In compiling this bibliography the author has used the earlier bibliographies of Birot and Roux (Hydroscopie et rabdomancie: Soc. agr., sci. ind. de Lyon Annales, 1912) and Klinckowstroem (Bibliographie der Wünschelrute, Munich, 1911). So far as possible the books cited have been examined at the Library of Congress and the citations verified.

15—. MELANCHTHON, PHILIPPE, Discours sur la sympathie [Discourse on sympathy (="sympathetic affinity")].

1532. BERNHARDUS, R. P., Vera atque brevis descriptio virgulae mercurialis, etc. [True yet brief description of the wand of Mercury, etc.], Prag.

1556. AGRICOLA, GEORGIUS, De re metallica [On metals], book 12, 1st ed.; another ed., Bâle, 1557. Translated into English by H. C. Hoover and L. H. Hoover, and published for the translators by the Mining Magazine, London, in 1912.

1569. BESSON, JACQUES, L'art et science de trouver les eaux et fontaines cachées sous terre [The art and science of finding water and fountains hidden under ground].

1569. PORTA, Jo. BAPTISTA, Magiae naturalis sive de miraculis rerum [Natural magic].

1573–1609. KECKERMANN, Systemata physica [Systematic physics], book 1, ch. 8.

1580. BODIN, J., La démonomanie des sorciers, ou le fléau des démons et des sorciers [The demonomania of sorcerers, or the plague of demons and sorcerers], book 1, ch. 5; 1st ed.

1584. PEUCER, GASPAR, Les devins [The diviners], book 13, ch. 10, pp. 145–146, Anvers.

1588. BELON, PIERRE, Les observations de plusieurs singularitez et choses memorables [Observations on many singular and remarkable things], book 1, ch. 50, p. 102.

1608. EGLIN, RAPHAËL. See Percis, Heliophilus.

1608. PERCIS, HELIOPHILUS A (Eglin, Raphaël), Disquisitio de Helia artista, in qua de metallorum transformatione, adversus Hagelii et Pererii Jesuitarum opiniones, evidenter et solide dissertur [Treatise on the Helian art, in which the transformation of metals, contrary to the views of Hagelius and Pererius, the Jesuits, is clearly and convincingly discussed], Marpurgi.

1617. LÖHNEYSS, GEORG E., Bericht vom Bergkwerck, wie man dieselben bauen und in guten Wolstandt bringen soll, sampt allen darzu gehörigen Arbeiten, Ordnung, und rechtlichen Process [Report on mines, how they are made and kept in good condition, together with all works, regulations, and laws pertaining thereto]. No place of publication (at the end: Zellerfeldt).

1618. LIGNARIDUS, HERMANN, Oblectamenta academica, etc. [Academic amusements], Oppenhemii.

1618. MONTANUS, ELIAS, Bergwerckschatz * * * [A treasury of mining lore], Frankfort on the Main.

1618. ROBERTI, JOH., Goclenius Heautontimorumenos [Goclenius, the self-tormentor], Luxemburg.

1619. GUTMANN, ÄGIDIUS, Offenbarung göttlicher Mayestät, etc. [Revelations of the Divine Majesty, etc.], Daschen.

1619. MAYER, MICHEL, Verum inventum [The truth discovered], ch. 4, Frankfort.

1626. BASILIUS VALENTINUS [Benedictine monk], Novum testamentum [New testament], French translation, book 2, ch. 22–28.

1630. GALIEN, CLAUDE, La découverte des eaux minérales de Château-Thierry et de leurs propriétés [The discovery of the mineral waters of Chateau-Thierry and their properties], Paris.

1632. BERTEREAU, MARTINE DE [Baroness Beausoleil], Veritable déclaration faite au Roy et à nos Seigneurs de son conseil des riches et inestimables trésors nouvellement descouverts dans le Royaume de France [True declaration made to the King and to our gentlemen of his Council concerning riches and inestimable treasures newly discovered in the kingdom of France]. No place of publication.

1632. BERTEREAU, MARTINE DE [Baroness Beausoleil], Veritable déclaration de la descouverte des mines et minières de France, par le moyen desquelles sa Majesté et ses subjects se peuvent passer de tous les pays estrangers; ensemble des propriétez d'aucunes sources et eaux minérales descouvertes depuis peu de temps à Château-Thierry. [True declaration of the discovery of mines and minerals of France, by means of which his Majesty and his subjects are able to surpass all foreign countries. Together with the properties of certain springs and mineral waters discovered a short time ago at Chateau-Thierry]. No place of publication.

1636. CAESIUS, BERNARD, Mineralogia [Mineralogy], book 1, ch. 7, sec. 4.

1636-1651. SCHWENTER, DANIEL, and GEORG PH. HARSDÖRFFER, Deliciae physicomathematicae * * * [Philosophical-mathematical recreations.] Nuremberg, 3 Bd., 6 Teil, 16 Frage.

1638. FLUDD, ROBERT (or FLUCTIBUS, ROBERT DE), Philosophia moysaica [The Mosaic philosophy], sec. 2, book 2, memb. 2, ch. 5, Gouda.

1639. PLATTES, GABRIEL, A discovery of subterraneall treasure, viz, of all manner of mines and minerals, from the gold to the coale; with plain directions and rules for the finding of them in all kingdoms and countries. Also the art of melting, refining, and assaying of them is plainly declared, so that every ordinary man, that is indifferently capacious, may with small charge presently try the value of such oares as shall be found either by rule or by accident, etc., London. Another edition, Philadelphia, 1792.

1640. BERTEREAU, MARTINE DE, La restitution de Pluton. À Mgr. l'éminentissime Cardinal Duc de Richelieu [The restitution of Pluto. To Mgr. the most eminent Cardinal Duc de Richelieu].

1645. KIRCHER, ATHANASIUS, Magnes, sive de arte magnetica [The magnet, or concerning the magnetic art], book 3, part 5, ch. 3, Rome.

1645. MOLINAEUS, PETRUS (Pierre du Moulin), Physicorum seu scientiae naturalis libri novem [Nine books of physics or natural science], 197 pp., Amsterdam. See book 5, ch. 7, pp. 81-82.

1648. ALDROVANDUS, ULYSSES, Musaeum metallicum [Museum of metals], book 1, ch. 1, art. Metallorum inveniendorum ratio, Bonn.

1654. FRANÇOIS, JEAN, La science des eaux, etc. [The science of water, etc.], Rennes and Paris.

1655. EICHHOLTZ, PETER, Geistliches Bergwerck, etc. [Spiritistic mining, etc.], Goslar.

1657-1659. SCHOTT, GASPAR, Magiae universalis naturae et artis, sive recondita naturalium et artificialium rerum scientia [The magic of nature and art, or occult science of natural and artificial things], 4 vols., Herbipoli.

1658. KLEIN, JACOBUS. See Sperling, Johann, et Jacobus Klein.

1658. SPERLING, JOHANN, et JACOBUS KLEIN, An virgula mercurialis agat ex occulta qualitate: disquisitio philosophica [Does the rod of Mercury act from occult power: a philosophical treatise], Wittenberg (about 1658).

1661. BEERN, P. C. See Liebentantz, Michael.

1661. BOYLE, ROBERT, Tentamina quaedam physiologica [Some physiologic experiments], London.

1661. LIEBENTANTZ, MICHAEL, et PHIL. CHRISTOPH BEERN, De magia baculorum; dissertatio physico-philologica [The magic of wands, a physical philologic dissertation], Wittenberg.

1662. RATTRAY, SYLVESTER, Theatrum sympatheticum auctum, exhibens varios
   authores * * * [A large "sympathetic" theater, exhibiting various
   authors], Nuremberg.
1665–1678. KIRCHER, ATHANASIUS, Mundus subterraneus, in XII libros digestus
   [The subterranean world, in 12 books], vol. 2, book 10, ch. 7, Amsterdam.
1665–1667. GLANVIL, JOSEPH [Reply to Robert Boyle's article. See Boyle, Robert,
   1661]: Philos. Trans., vol. 2, Nos. 28 and 39, in the Savoy (London).
1666. BUTSCHKY VON RUTINFELD, SAMUEL, Erweiterte und verbässerte Hoch-
   Deutsche Kanzelley, etc. [Broadened and improved high German preaching
   (containing mention of the divining rod)], Breslau and Jena.
1667. PRAETORIUS, JOHANN, Gazophylaci Gaudium. Das ist Ein Ausbund von
   Wündschel-Ruthen oder sehr lustreiche und ergetzliche Historien von wun-
   derseltzamen Erfindungen der Schätze, etc. [The joy of the treasurer—that
   is, a pattern of divining rod or very pleasurable and entertaining history of
   most strange discoveries of treasures], Leipsic.
1669. KIRCHMAIER, THEODOR, et J. H. MARTIUS, Dissertatio physica de virgula
   divinatrice [Philosophic treatise on the divining rod], Wittenberg.
1669. PRAETORIUS, JOHANN, Der Abentheuerliche Glücks-Topf * * * [The
   strange luck pot * * *].
1671. WEBSTER, JOHN, Metallographia: or, an history of metals. Wherein is declared
   the signs of ores and minerals both before and after digging, the causes and
   manner of their generations, their kinds, sorts, and differences; with the
   description of sundry new metals, or semimetals, and many other things
   pertaining to mineral knowledge, etc., London [pp. 104–110 on the divining rod, which the author condemns].
1671. WILLENIUS, MATTHAEUS, or WILLE, MATTHES, De salis origine * * * tractatus philosophicus [On the origin of salt, a philosophic treatise], Jena, 1671;
   new edition, 1684.
1673. SCHWIMMER, JOHANN M., Tractatus physicus * * * [Treatise on philoso-
   phy], Jena. 4°. Diss. 8, pp. 129–134.
1674. ANHORN, BARTHOLOM, Magiologia, Basel.
1674. DECHALES, CL.-FR. MILLET, Cursus seu mundus mathematicus [General course
   in mathematics], 4 vols., Lyons 1674. 2d ed., Lugduni, 1690. De fontibus
   et fluviis [Concerning springs and streams], vol. 3, tractatus 17.
1674. LE ROYER, JACQUES, Traité du baston universel [Treatise on the universal
   rod], Rouen.
1674. SCHAUB, J. D., Dissertatio physica de virgula mercuriali, quam divina aspirante
   gratia, etc. [Philosophic treatise on the rod of mercury, which divine favor,
   etc.], Marpurgi Cattorum.
1675. FROMMANN, JOANNES CHRISTIAN, Tractatus de fascinatione novus et singularis
   [A new and remarkable treatise on enchantment], Nuremberg.
1676. SCHWIMMER, M. J. M., Kurtzweiliger und physicalischer Zeitvertreiber
   * * * [Amusing and physical pastime * * *], 2 parts, Jena (Theod.
   Fleischer). Part 1, pp. 219–230.
1677. PRAETORIUS, JOHANN, Philologemata abstrusa de pollice; * * * [Hidden
   wisdom of the thumb], Sagani et Lipsiae.
1678. FRATTA ET MONTALBANO, March, MARCO ANTONIO DELLA, Pratica minerale.
   [Containing in chapter 2]: De segni per ritrovar le miniere [The signs for
   finding minerals], Bologna.
1678. LE ROYER, JACQUES, Oeuvres de Messire. Contains, pp. 226–359, Traité des
   influences, etc. [Treatise on influences, etc.], Paris.
1679. BUTSCHKY VON RUTINFELD, SAMUEL, Wohl-Bebauter Rosen-Thal, etc. [Well-
   made rose valley], Nuremberg. Contains, pp. 728–731, reference to the
   divining rod.

1679 and 1684. SAINT-ROMAIN, G. B. DE, Physica sive scientia naturalis scholasticis tricis liberata [Physics or natural science freed from scholastic trivialities], Lugduni-Batav.

1680. MELTZER VON WOLCKENSTEIN, CHRISTIAN, De Hermundurorum metallurgia argentaria * * * [On the silver metallurgy of the Hermunduri], Leipzig.

1681. LEBENWALDT, ADAM VON, Fünfftes Tractätl, von dess Teuffels List und Betrug in der Berg-Ruethen und Berg-Spiegl [Fifth tract, on the devil's cunning and deceit in the mining rod and mining mirror], Saltzburg.

1682. HOHBERG, WOLFF HELMH. VON, Georgica curiosa, Das ist umständlicher Bericht und klarer Unterricht von dem adelichen Land- und Feld-Leben, etc. [that is, a detailed account and clear information concerning the nobility of country and peasant life], Nuremberg, 2 vols.; vol. 1, ch. 76, p. 76.

1684. SAINT-ROMAIN. See Saint-Romain, G. B. de, 1679.

1684. SCHULTZ, THOMAS JOHANN, Des Teuffels Bergwerck; vom Schatzgraben [The devil's mining; from the treasure diggings], Wittenberg.

1689. KIRCHMANN, M. C., Virtutem virgulae saliaris * * * [The power of the divining rod], Wittenberg.

1689-1702. SZENT-IVANY, MARTIN, Curiosiora et selectiora variarum scientiarum miscellanea * * * [Curious and select miscellanies of various sciences], 3 vols. Tyrnaviae. See vol. 1, p. 179.

1691-1693. BEKKER, BALTHASAR, De betoverde Weereld, etc. [The bewitched world], Amsterdam.

1692. CHAUVIN, PIERRE, Lettre à Mme. la marquise de Senozan, sur les moyens dont on s'est servi pour découvrir les complices d'un assassinat commis à Lyon, le 5 juillet, 1692 [Letter to Madam la marquise de Senozan, on the means employed to discover the accomplices in an assassination committed at Lyons July 5, 1692], Lyons.

1692. GARNIER, PIERRE, Dissertation physique [Philosophic treatise, in the form of a letter to M. de Séve, Sr. de Fléchères, in which it is proved that the extraordinary faculties by which Jacques Aymar, with a divining rod, followed murderers and robbers, discovered water and buried silver, reestablished landmarks, etc., depended on a very ordinary natural cause], Lyons.

1692. PANTHOT, JEAN-BAPTISTE, Lettre de M. Panthot, doien du Collège des médicins de Lyon, écrite à Messire Antoine Daquin, conseiller du Roy * * *, sur un assassinat des plus énormes, commis à Lyon le 5 juillet 1692, et les moyens que l'on a pris pour découvrir les autheurs [Letter of M. Panthot, dean of the college of medicine of Lyons, to M. Antoine Daquin, adviser to the King, in regard to a horrible murder committed at Lyons July 5, 1692, and the means employed for discovering the criminals], no place of publication or date (1692?).

1693. BEKKER, BALTHASAR, Die bezauberte Welt, etc. [The bewitched world, etc.], Amsterdam.

1693. BUNTING, J. P., Sylva subterranea [Subterranean woodland, or the admirable usefulness of subterranean coal beds, etc.], Halle.

1693. CHATELAIN, Prof. (?), Dissertation physique, dans laquelle il est démontré clairement que les talens qu'on attribue à l'homme à baguette * * * sont tous talens supposez [Philosophic treatise, in which it is shown clearly that the talents attributed to the diviner * * * are all imaginary], Grenoble.

1693. COMIERS, CLAUDE, La baguette justifiée et ses effets demontrez naturels [The divining rod justified and its action shown to be natural]: Mercure galant, March.

1693. COMIERS, CLAUDE, Reponse à l'anonime [Reply to an anonymous article]: Mercure galant, August.

1693. GARNIER, PIERRE, Histoire de la baguette de Jacques Aymar pour faire toutes sortes de découvertes [History of the divining rod of Jacques Aymar, for making all sorts of discoveries], Lyons.

1693. G., E. F., Lettre concernant la divination par la baguette [Letter concerning divination by means of the divining rod], à Comiers: Mercure galant, March.

1693. LA GARDE, Abbé de, Dissertation physique, dans laquelle il est démontré clairement que les talens qu'on attribue à l'homme à baguette * * * sont tous talens supposez [Philosophical treatise, in which it is clearly shown that the faculties attributed to the diviner * * * are all imaginary], Grenoble.

1693. LEBRUN, PIERRE, Lettres qui découvrent l'illusion des philosophes sur la baguette, et qui détruisent leurs systèmes [Letters which expose the illusion of philosophers in regard to the divining rod and which destroy their systems]. Published anonymously, Paris, 1693; Amsterdam, 1696.

1693. LE LORRAIN, Abbé. See Vallemout, Abbé de, 1693.

1693. Lettre sur la physique occulte de la baguette divinatoire [Letter on the occult physics of the divining rod]: Mercure galant, April.

1693. NICOLAS, JEAN, of Grenoble, La verge de Jacob, ou l'art de trouver les trésors, les sources, les limites, les métaux, les mines, les minéraux et autres choses cachées, par l'usage du bâton fourché [The rod of Jacob, or the art of finding treasures, springs, boundaries, metals, mines, minerals, and other hidden things, by the use of the forked twig], Lyons.

1693. PANTHOT, JEAN-BAPTISTE, Traité de la baguette ou la recherche des véritables usages auxquels elle convient, etc. [Treatise on the divining rod, or the investigation of genuine uses to which it is adapted, etc.], Lyons.

1693. RENAUD, ANDRÉ, Réponse aux objections * * * [Response to the objections * * *], Lyons.

1693. RENAUD, ANDRÉ, Critique sincère de plusieurs écrits sur la fameuse baguette * * * [Sincere criticism of many writings on the famous divining rod * * *], Lyons.

1693. VAGNY, DE, Histoire merveilleuse d'un maçon qui, conduit par la baguette divinatoire, a suivi un meurtrier pendant quarante-cinque heures sur la terre et plus de trente heures sur l'eau [Marvelous story of a mason who, led by a divining rod, followed a murderer for forty-five hours over land and for more than thirty hours over water], Grenoble, about 1693?

1693. VALLEMONT, Abbé de (Pierre Le Lorrain), La physique occulte, ou Traité de la baguette divinatoire [Occult philosophy, or treatise on the divining rod], many editions, Paris.

1693-94. TENTZEL, WILHELM E., Monatliche Unterredungen einiger guten Freunde von allerhand Büchern und andern annehmlichen Geschichten * * * [Monthly conferences of some good friends of various books and other acceptable narratives * * *], Leipzig.

1694. BUSSIÈRE, PAUL, Lettre à M. l'abbé D. L. sur les véritables effets de la baguette de Jacques Aymar [Letter to M. the Abbé D. L. on the true effects of Jacques Aymar's rod], Paris.

1694. LE CONTE, J. GEORG. See Zentgravius, D. J. J., and J. G. Le Conte, 1694.

1694. MÉNESTRIER, CL.-FR., La philosophie des images énigmatiques * * * [The philosophy of enigmatic appearances], Lyons.

1694. OZANAM, J., Récréations mathématiques et physiques * * * [Mathematical and philosophic diversions * * *] [see problem 35: To determine the places in the earth where springs occur, and problem 36: To determine the places in the earth where minerals and treasures are hidden], 2 vols., Paris.

1694. VIOLET, P., Traité en forme de lettre contre la nouvelle rhabdomancie ou la manière nouvelle de deviner avec une baguette fourchûe. Dans lequel on réfute tout ce qu'on a écrit pour en justifier l'usage [Treatise in the form of a letter opposing the new rhabdomancy or the new manner of divining with the forked twig, in which all that has been written to justify its adoption is refuted], Lyons.

1694. ZENTGRAVIUS, DAN. JOH. JOACH., et JOH. GEORG LE CONTE, Ex legibus Ebraeorum forensibus contra magiam de divinationibus magicis: eaque occasione de virgula divina et divinatione nupera Jacobi Aymari, Delphinatis, sicariorum et furum investigandorum causa facta [The public laws of the Hebrews against magical divination, and the use of the divining rod in recent divination by (Jacques) Aymar of Delphinas [the diviner?] for the purpose of discovering assassins and thieves], Argentorati. Pp. 22–28 on the divining rod.

1696. RABUS, PIETER, article in De Boekzaal van Europe, vol. 9, pp. 152–156, P. Rabus, publisher.

1697. BAYLE, PIERRE, Dictionnaire historique et critique [Historical and critical dictionary], article "Abaris," vol. 4, Rotterdam.

1697. ETTNER, JOH. CHR., Des getreuen Eckharts unwürdiger Doctor, in welchem wie ein Medicus, der rechtschaffen handeln will, beschaffen seyn soll, etc. [paper on the moral qualifications of a physician], Augsburg and Leipzig.

1697. LEDEL, SIGISM., De virgula metallica [Concerning the metallic wand]: Miscellanea curiosa sive Ephemer. medico-physic. Germanic. Acad. Caesaro-Leopold. curiosorum, Frankfort and Leipzig.

1697–1722. STURM, J. C., Physica electiva sive hypothetica [Select or hypothetical physics], 2 vols. Nuremberg, see vol. 2.

1700. RÖSSLER, B.,. Speculum metallurgiae politissimum * * * [Mirror of metallurgy], Dresden.

1700. TOLLIUS, J., Epistolae itinerariae * * * [Letters of travel], Amsterdam.

1700. ZEIDLER, JOHANN GOTTFRIED, Pantomysterium, oder das Neue vom Jahre in der Wünschelruthe, als einem allgemeinen Werckzeuge menschlicher verborgenen Wissenschaft [Pantomysterium (all mystery), or news of the year concerning the divining rod as a universal tool of knowledge hidden from man], Hall in Magdeburg.

1702. LEBRUN, PIERRE, Histoire critique des pratiques superstitieuses, qui ont séduit le peuple et embarassé les sçavans. Avec la méthode et les principes pour discerner les effets naturels d'avec ceux qui ne le sont pas, par un prêtre de l'Oratoire [Critical history of superstitious practices which have seduced the people and embarrassed the learned, with the method of distinguishing natural powers from those which are not natural, by a priest of the Oratory], 3 parts. Rouen, 1701; parts 1 and 2 treat of the divining rod. Same work, 3 vols., Paris, 1732. Reprinted in Holland (3 vols.) in 1732 and (4 vols.) in 1736.

1703. BECCHER, JOACHIM, Physica subterranea [Subterranean physics], book 1, sect. 7, No. 20, Leipsic.

1703. VAGEDES, HENR., Opera academica, quae seorsim antehac edita in unum corpus collegit * * * [Academic papers issued separately, now collected into one work], Frankfort and Leipzig.

1704. ALBINUS, THEOPHIL., Das entlarvete Idolum der Wünschel-Ruthe [The exposed idolatry of the divining rod], Dresden. A dissertation against the rod, published with the approval of the faculty of Protestant theology of Leipzig.

1704. WEISE, J. M. *See* Albinus, Theophil.

1704–1714. VALENTINI, D. M. B., Museum museorum * * * [Museum of museums], Frankfort on the Main.

1705. Rivinus, Quint. Sept. Flor., Enunciata iuris, ad ordinationem processus iudiciarii Saxonici electoralem collecta * * * [Pronouncements of law. Saxon judicial judgments collected by electoral order], Leipzig.

1706. Albinus, Theophile, Kurtze Fortsetzung des entlarvten Idoli der Wünschel-Ruthe, etc. [Short treatise on the idolatry of the divining rod, etc.], Dresden.

1709. Pfungst, Oskar, Zur Psychologie der Wünschelruthe [On the psychology of the divining rod]: Deutsche Revue, 34th year, Stuttgart and Leipsic.

1712. Vilbussière, Le Commandeur de, Discours du boiteux sur la baguette divinatoire * * * [Discourse of the lame man (Comiers?) on the divining rod * * *], Amsterdam.

1716. Rohr, Bernhard von, Compendieuse Haushaltungsbibliothek * * * [Householder's abridged library], Leipzig.

1719. Fischer, Joh. Andr., Facultatis medicae in perantiqua electorali ad hieram academia decanus et senior, D. Joh. Andreas Fischer * * * lectori benevolo S. P. D. ipsique de complemento votorum suorum solicito virgulam divinatoriam porrigit, Erfordiae.

1719-1724. Flemming, Hanns Friedr. von, Der vollkommene teutsche Jäger, etc. [The complete German hunter], Leipzig.

1725. Saint-André, De, Lettres de M. de St. André [to a friend on the subject of magic, etc.], Paris.

1726. Walch, J. G., Philosophisches Lexicon * * * [Philosophic lexicon * * *], Leipzig.

1726-1740. Feyjoo, B. G. See Feyjoo, Benito-Geronymo, 1740.

1728. Loescher, Martin Gotthelf, Physica theoretica et experimentalis, etc. [Theoretic and experimental physics, etc.], Wittenberg.

1728. Schmidt, J. G., Die zu guter Stunde ausgeheckte curieuse Grillen * * * [The opportunity hatched, curious vagaries * * *], Chemnitz.

1731. Lavaur, De, Histoire de la fable conférée avec l'histoire sainte. Où l'on voit que les grandes fables, le culte et les mystères du paganisme ne sont que des copies altérées des histoires, des usages et des traditions des Hébreux [The history of mythology compared with sacred history. In which it is seen that the great myths, worship, and the mysteries of paganism are merely modified imitations of the histories, customs, and traditions of the Hebrews], vol. 2, pp. 152-161, Amsterdam.

1733. Lebrun, Pierre, Superstitions anciennes et modernes, etc. [Ancient and modern superstitions, etc.], Amsterdam.

1734. Wernher, J. F., and F. F. Rivinus, Dissertatio inauguralis de finibus per virgulam mercurialem non investigandis. Von Aufsuchung der Grentzen durch Wünschel-Ruthen, [Inaugural essay on limits not to be investigated by the divining rod], Wittenberg.

1736-1742. Wegner, G. W., Schau-Platz vieler ungereimten Meynungen und Erzehlungen [Theater of many absurd opinions and reports], Berlin.

1737-1753. Bélidor, Bernard Forest de, Architecture hydraulique, etc. [Hydraulic architecture, etc.], 2 vols., Paris. Another edition in 4 vols. published in Paris in 1810.

1737. Braüner, J. J., Physicalisch- und historisch-erörterte Curiositäten, etc. [Curiosities philosophically and historically considered], Frankfort.

1740. Bluhme, Joh. Barth. See Dethardingius and Bluhme.

1740. Bruhier d'Ablaincourt, J. J., Caprices d'imagination, ou lettres sur différens sujets d'histoire, etc. [Caprices of the imagination, or letters on different historical subjects, etc.], Paris.

1740. Dethardingius, Georg, and J. B. Bluhme, Novam scrutationem negotii physico-magici per virgulam vacillantem detegendi occulta * * * [A new examination of the physico-magical business of detecting hidden things by the divining rod], Hafniae.

1740. FEYJOO, BENITO-GERONYMO, Theatro critico universal, etc. [Universal forum for criticism], 9 vols., Madrid, 1726–1740.

1741. STOER, JOHANN GOTTLIEB, De privilegio metallicorum commentatio [Commentary on the law of metals], pp. 36–37, Erfordiae.

1746. KRÜGER, JOHANN GOTTLOB, Geschichte der Erde in den allerältesten Zeiten [History of the earth in the most ancient times], Halle.

1747. KIESSLING, JOHANN GOTTFRIED, Gegründete Nachricht von dem Bergbau und Schmelzwesen in der Grafschaft Mannssfeld * * * etc. [Authentic information on the mining and smelting in Mannssfeld County * * * etc.], p. 97, Leipzig.

1751. COOKWORTHY, WILLIAM, Observations on the properties and use of the virgula divina: Gentleman's Mag. and Hist. Chronicle, London.

1751–1753. MYLIUS, CHR., Physikalische Belustigungen [Diversions in philosophy] 3 vols., Berlin.

1753. KÄSTNER, A. G., article in Hamburgisches Magazin, vol. 4, pt. 1, p. 41, Hamburg.

1756. EYSSVOGEL, FRIDERICH GOTTLOB, Neu-eröffnetes Magazin * * *, vol. 1, ch. 38, Von etlichen Wasser-Künsten. Wie man Wasserquellen suchen und finden solle [Newly published magazine. * * * Of sundry water arts. How one should search for and find springs of water], Bamberd.

1757. SCHÜTZE, HEINRICH CARL, Vernunft- und schriftmässige Abhandlung von Aberglauben. * * * [Rational and scriptural treatment of superstition * * *], pp. 218–222, Wernigerode.

1757. WALLERIUS, J. G., et J. L. ROMAN, Kort Afhandling om Malmgångars Upsökande * * * [Short treatise on the investigation of ore deposits], Upsala.

1763. FEUDIVIRUS, H. F., Gebrauch der Berg- und Wünschel-Ruthe, etc. [Use of the ore- and divining-rod, etc.], Leipzig.

1770. ALEMBERT, JEAN BAPTISTE LE ROND D', and DENIS DIDEROT, Encyclopédie, ou dictionnaire raisonné des sciences, des arts et des métiers [Encyclopedia or analytical dictionary of sciences, arts, and trades], articles on Source, Baguette divine, Rabdomancie, etc., Geneva. New ed., 1777.

1772. Histoire véritable et merveilleuse d'une jeune anglaise * * * [The true and marvelous story of an English girl * * * hydroscope * * *], Paris.

1772. LALANDE, J. J. DE, Lettre sur le prétendu hydroscope [Letter on the so-called hydroscope (Paraogue)]: Le Mercure de France, July 2, pp. 169–173.

1772. SAURI, Abbé, L'hydroscope et le ventriloque [The hydroscope and the ventriloquist], Amsterdam and Paris.

1773. CANCRINUS, F. L., Erste Gründe der Berg- und Salzwerkskunde [First principles of mining and of the salt industry], Frankfort, 12 parts, 1773–1791. See part 3 (1773), pp. 26–40.

1773. JUGEL, JOHANN GOTTFRIED, Geometria subterranea, etc. [Underground surveying, etc.], Leipzig.

1777–1778. KELLER, ERNST URBAN, Das Grab des Aberglaubens [The grave of superstition], Frankfort and Leipzig.

1778. PRYCE, WILLIAM, Mineralogia Cornubiensis; a treatise on minerals, mines, and mining, etc., London. See pp. 113–124.

1779. GOBET, Les anciens minéralogistes du royaume de France [The ancient mineralogists of the kingdom of France], 2 vols., Paris. See vol. 1.

1781. FORMEY, J. H. S., Baguette divinatoire [The divining rod]: Dictionnaire des merveilles de la nature, by Sigaud de la Fond, 2 vols., Paris. See vol. 1, p. 75.

1781. THOUVENEL, PIERRE, Mémoire physique et médicinal, montrant des rapports
— évidents entre les phénomènes de la baguette divinatoire, du magnétisme
animale et de l'électricité [Physical and medical memoir showing the evident relations between the phenomena of the divining rod and animal magnetism and electricity], Paris and London.

1782. ARCET, J. D' [et al.], Observations faites sur la vertu de Bleton de sentir l'impression des eaux souterraines coulantes [Observations on the ability of Bleton
to feel the impression of flowing underground waters]: Jour. de Paris, No.
177, June 26, pp. 719–726.

1782. DÉYEUX, [Experiments with Bleton]: Jour. de Paris, No. 230, Aug. 18, pp.
939–941.

1782. GUILLOTIN. See Arcet, J. d', et al.

1782. HUVIER, DUMÉE, article in Jour. de Paris, No. 249, Sept. 6, pp. 1015–1017.

1782. LALANDE, J. J. DE, Lettre sur la baguette divinatoire de Bleton [Letter on the
divining rod of Bleton]: Journal des sçavans.

1782. LORTHE, G. A. DE, L'art de faire tourner la baguette divinatoire [The art of
causing the divining rod to turn], Paris.

1782. LORTHE, G. A. DE, Mélanges d'opuscules mathématiques [Miscellany of short
mathematical papers], Paris. New ed., 1785.

1782. MACQUER. See Arcet, J. d', et al.

1782. MITOUART. See Arcet, J. d', et al.

1782. POISSONIER. See Arcet, J. d', et al.

1782. THOUVENEL. See Arcet, J. d', et al.

1784–1791. DECREMPS, La magie blanche dévoilée * * * avec des réflexions sur
la baguette divinatoire, etc. [White magic exposed * * * with some
reflections on the divining rod, etc.], 3 vols., Paris. See vol. 1, p. 49.

1784. LORTHE, G. A. DE, Mélanges d'opuscules mathématiques. Lettre à M.
Thouvenel [Miscellany of short mathematical papers], Paris.

1784. THOUVENEL, PIERRE, Second mémoire physique et médical [Second physical
and medical memoir], London and Paris.

1784. THOUVENEL, PIERRE, Extrait du journal des voyages et des expériences de
Bleton [Extract from the journal of the journeys and experiments of Bleton]:
Jour. de Paris.

1785. Découverte des eaux d'Uriage par la baguette magique du sorcier Bleton [Dis-
covery of the waters of Uriage by the magic wand of the sorcerer Bleton]:
Jour. historique et politique de Genève, Jan. 8.

1785. ROZIER, Abbé, Cours complet ou dictionnaire universel d'agriculture [Com
plete course or universal dictionary of agriculture], Paris.

1785. STERZINGER, FERDINAND, Bemühung den Aberglaube zu stürzen [The effort
to overthrow superstition], chap. 24, pp. 89–92, Munich.

1785. TREBRA, F. W. H. VON, Erfahrungen vom Innern der Gebirge, nach Beobachtungen gesammlet und herausgegeben [Knowledge of the interior of mountains based on observations gathered and published], Dessau and Leipzig.

1786. HALLE, J. S., Magie, oder die Zauberkräfte der Natur, so auf den Nutzen und die
Belustigung angewandt worden [Magic, or the magic virtues of nature, as they
were applied in practical use and in amusement], Berlin.

1786. NICOLAS, M., Mémoires sur les maladies épidémiques qui ont regné dans la province de Dauphiné dépuis l'an 1780. Avec des observations sur les eaux
minérales, sur l'histoire naturelle de cette province, et quelques consulta-
tions de médicine [Memoires on the epidemic maladies which have prevailed
in the province of Dauphine since the year 1780. With some observations
on the mineral waters, on the natural history of that province, and some
medical advice], Grenoble.

1790-91. ECKARTSHAUSEN, KARL VON, Aufschlüsse zur Magie aus geprüften Erfahrungen über verborgene philosophische Wissenschaften, etc. [Revelation of magic through proved experiences in occult philosophy], Munich.

1790. LUCE, J. W. L., Bemerkungen und Muthmassungen über die Wünschelruthe, etc. [Observations and conjectures on the divining rod, etc.], Neuwied and Leipzig.

1790. REGNARD, JEAN F., Oeuvres complètes [Complete works], 6 vols., Paris, 1790. New ed., Paris, 1820. Vol. 6, pp. 73-98, contains "La baguette de Vulcain, Comédie."

1791. CANCRINUS. See Cancrinus, F. L., 1773.

1791. FISCHER, H. L., Das Buch vom Aberglauben [The book of superstitions], Leipzig.

1791. FORTIS, Abbé A., Lettera del Abbé Fortis al Sign. Abbé Lazaro Spallanzani sugli sperimenti di Pennet [Letter from Abbe Fortis to Signor Abbé Lazaro Spallanzani on the experiments of Pennet]: Opuscoli scelti sulle scienze e sulle arti, vol. 14, Milan.

1791. SPALLANZANI, Abbé LAZARO, Lettera del Sign. Abbé Spallanzani al Sign. Abbé Fortis [Letter from Spallanzani to Fortis concerning the experiments with Pennet]: Opuscoli scelti sulle scienze e sulle arti, vol. 14, Milan.

1791. FABRIONI, G. V. M., Vera vera verissima relazione dei fatti e detti della bacchetta divinatoria, del suo primo avvento alla sua morte in Toscana [A strictly true account of the promises and performance of the divining rod from its first performance to its last in Tuscany], Florence.

1792. THOUVENEL, PIERRE, Résumé sur les expériences d'électrométrie souterraine (Summary of the experiments on underground electrometry]: vol. 1, Milan; vol. 2, Brescia.

1793. AMORETTI, CARLO, Istoria breve [Brief history]. Lettera del Sign. Abbé Carlo Amoretti al P. Prof. Francesco Soave su alcune sperienze electtriche [Letter from Signor Abbe Carlo Amoretti to P. Prof. Francesco Soave in regard to certain electrical experiments (concerning Pennet, the water finder)]: Opuscoli scelti sulle scienze e sulle arti, vol. 16, Milan.

1793. RAMANZINI, DIONIGI, Esperienze eseguite da Pennet in Verona nel mese di Giuglio, 1793 [Experiments performed by Pennet in Verona in the month of July, 1793], Verona.

1793. SPADONI, PAOLO, Lettera idroelettrica sull' esperienze di un secondo Pennet (Petroselli) [Hydroelectric letter concerning the experiments of a second Pennet (Petroselli), Ancona.

1793. SPALLANZANI, Abbé LAZARE, Lettera dell' Abbate Spallanzani al Signor Thouvenel [Letter from Abbé Spallanzani to Mr. Thouvenel]: Annali di chimica e storia naturale, etc., Pavia.

1793. THOUVENEL, PIERRE, Nouvelles pièces relatives à l'électricité organique [New papers relative to organic electricity], Vicenza.

1795. LICHTENBERG, G. C., und J. H. VOIGT, Magazin für das Neuste aus der Physik und Naturgeschichte, 10 vols., Gotha. See article 1, pp. 144-159.

1796. AMORETTI, CARLO, Su vari individui che hanno la facolta di sentire le sorgenti, le miniere, etc. [Concerning various individuals who possess the faculty of sensing springs, minerals, etc.]: Opuscoli scelti sulle scienze e sulle arti, vol. 19, Milan.

1796. HALLE, J. S., Fortgesetzte Magie, oder die Zauberkräfte der Natur, so auf den Nutzen und die Belustigung angewandt worden [Magic explained, or the magic virtues of nature as they were applied in practical use and in amusement], 8 vols., Berlin. See pp. 446-458.

1798. AMORETTI, CARLO, Ricerche storico-fisiche sulla rabdomanzia, ossia sulla elettro-metria sotteranea [Historical-physical researches on rhabdomancy, or on subterranean electrometry]: Opuscoli scelti sulle scienze e sulle arti, vol. 20, Milan.

1798. WIEGLEB, J. C., Die natürliche Magie aus allerhand belustigenden und nützlichen Kunststücken bestehend [Natural magic existing in various amusing and useful tricks], Berlin and Stettin.

1800. Lettre de M. J. M. C. à M. de Salgues [editor of the Journal des spectacles, on the divining rod]. No place or date (about 1800).

1800. WENZEL, G. J., Dramatisirte Erzählungen aus dem Gebiete des Wunderbaren * * * [Dramatized narratives from the realm of the wonderful * * *], Leipzig.

1801. AMORETTI, CARLO, Ricerche storiche sulla rabdomanzia [Historical researches on rhabdomancy]: Opuscoli scelti sulle scienze e sulle arti, vol. 21, Milan.

1802. FORTIS, Abbé ALBERT, Mémoires pour servir à l'histoire naturelle et principalement à l'oryctographie de l'Italie et des pays adjacens [Memoirs on the natural history and oryctography of Italy and adjacent countries], 2 vols., Paris. See vol. 2, pp. 138-283.

1802. THOUVENEL, PIERRE, La guerra di dieci anni [The 10-year war], Verona.

1802-1806. WEINHOLT, A., Heilkraft des thierischen Magnetismus nach eigenen Beobachtungen [Healing by means of animal magnetism according to personal observations], 3 vols., Lemgo, vol. 3, pt. 1, p. 283, 1805.

1803. ARNIM, L. A. VON, Neuere Beobachtungen über sogenannte untererdische Elektrometrie [New observations on the so-called underground electrometry]: Annalen der Physik, vol. 13, Halle.

1804. AMORETTI, CARLO, [Miscellaneous letters on rhabdomancy]: Nuova scelta d'opuscoli interessanti sulle scienze e sulle arti, vol. 1, Milan.

1806. AMORETTI, CARLO, Dell' azione di varie sostanze sobra altre sostenute pendenti su di esse sperimenti del fu Alberto Fortis, etc. [Of the action of various substances supported above others, based on experiments made by the late Alberto Fortis]: Soc. ital. delle scienza,Mem., vol. 13, Modena.

1806. FORTIS, Abbé ALBERT, Mémoire sur les pendules électromètres [Memoir on electrometer pendulums]: Soc. ital. sci. exactes Bull., vol. 13.

1806. THOUVENEL, PIERRE, Mélanges d'histoire naturelle, de physique et de chimie; mémoires sur l'aérologie et l'électrologie [Miscellanies of natural history, physics, and chemistry; memoirs on aerology and electrology], 3 vols., Paris. See vols. 2 and 3.

1807. ARETIN, C. F. VON, Beyträge zur litterärischen Geschichte der Wünschelruthe [Contributions to the literary history of the divining rod], Munich.

1807. PAOLI, P., Sperimenti col pendolo [Experiments with the pendulum]: Nuova scelta d'opuscoli interessanti sulle scienze e sulle arti, vol. 2, Milan.

1807. SCHELLING, F. W. J. VON, article in Allgemeine Litteratur-Zeitung, Jena.

1808. AMORETTI, CARLO, Della rabdomanzia ossia elettrometria animale. Ricerche fisiche e storiche [On rhabdomancy or animal electrometry. Physical and historical researches], Milan.

1808. EBEL, JOHANN GOTTFRIED, Über den Bau der Erde in dem Alpen-Gebirge, etc. [On the geologic structure of the Alps], 2 vols., Zurich. See vol. 2, p. 392.

1808. GERBOIN, Dr., Recherches expérimentales sur un nouveau mode de l'action électrique [Experimental researches on a new mode of electrical action], Strasburg.

1808. GILBERT, L. W., Kritische Aufsätze über die in München wieder erneuerten Versuche mit Schwefelkiespendeln und Wünschelruthen [Critical essay on the renewed experiments in Munich with magic pendulums and divining rods], Halle.

1808. RITTER, WILHELM, Der Siderismus [Magnetic treatment], Tübingen.

1810. SALGUES, J. B., Des erreurs et préjugés répandus dans les diverses classes de la société [Errors and prejudices peculiar to different classes of society], 3 vols., Paris. 5th ed., Brussels, 1847, vol. 1, pp. 81–90, Divining rod (by Coudrier).

1810. SEMENTINI, LUIGI, Pensieri e sperimenti sulla bacchetta divinatoria [Thoughts and experiments on the divining rod], Naples.

1810. STEFFENS, HEINRICH, Geognostisch-geologische Aufsätze [Geologic treatises], pp. 315–316, 319–320, Hamburg.

1810. ZOLLIKOFER, Dr., Rhabdomantische Versuche [Rhabdomantic experiments]: Cotta's Morgenblatt für gebildete Stände, 4th year, Tübingen.

1811. FLÖRKE, H. GUSTAV, Repertorium des Neuesten und Wissenswürdigsten aus der gesamten Naturkunde [Reportory of the newest and best things in natural science], Berlin.

1811. KLUGE, CARL A. F., Versuch einer Darstellung des animalischen Magnetismus als Heilmittel [Investigation of an exhibition of animal magnetism as a means of healing], Berlin. Divining rod, p. 296.

1814. PHILLIPS, W., article in Geol. Soc. London Trans., vol. 2.

1816. AMORETTI, CARLO, Elementi di elettrometria animale, etc. [Elements of animal electrometry], Milan.

1816. GINSBERG, FR., Rabdomantische Sensibilität [Rhabdomantic sensibility]: Archiv der Medicin, Chirurgie und Pharmazie, 1st year, Aarau.

1818. OKEN, L., Isis, oder encyclopädische Zeitung [Isis, or encyclopedic newspaper], p. 140, Jena.

1818. ZSCHOKKE, HEINRICH, Überlieferungen zur Geschichte unserer Zeit [Contributions to the history of our time], 2d year, pp. 331–335, Aarau.

1819. VOSS, LUDWIG VON, [On the divining rod]: Jahrbücher für den Lebensmagnetismus, oder Neues Askläpieion, 2 vols., Berlin. See vol. 1, pp. 121, 134.

1819. WEISSE, J. FR., Erfahrungen über arzneiverständige Somnambulen, nebst einigen Versuchen mit einer Wasserfühlerin [Experiences with somnambulists skilled in medical science, together with some experiments with a water feeler], Berlin.

1820. CUVILLERS, ÉTIENNE FÉLIX, Baron D'HÉNIN DE, Le magnétisme éclairé, ou introduction aux archives du magnétisme animal [Magnetism explained, or introduction to records of animal magnetism].

1820. HUFELAND, C. W., articles in Journal der practischen Heilkunde, Berlin.

1821. D'OUTREPONT, Prof., [On J. P. Brayer, diviner]: Zeitschrift für psychische Ärzte, Leipzig, pt. 1, pp. 94–109.

1821. PASSAVANT, JOH. CARL, Untersuchungen über den Lebensmagnetismus und das Hellsehen [Investigations of animal magnetism and clairvoyance], Frankfort on the Main.

1822. KIESER, D. G., System des Tellurismus, oder thierischen Magnetismus [System of the earth or animal magnetism], 2 vols., Leipzig. See vol. 1, pp. 161–176, on the divining rod and magic pendulum.

1825. COLLIN DE PLANCY [Abbé MIGNE], Dictionnaire infernal, Baguette divinatoire [divining rod], 2d ed., vol. 1, pp. 305–311, Paris. 4th ed., Brussels, 1845.

1826. LOCKHART, M., Rapport fait au nom de la section d'histoire naturelle sur l'ouvrage de M. le comte de Tristan, intitulé Recherches sur quelques effluves terrestres [Report made in the name of the section of natural history on the work of the Count de Tristan, entitled Researches on some terrestrial emanations]: Soc. roy. sci., belles lettres et arts d'Orléans Annales, vol. 8, pp. 82–88, Orleans.

1826. TRISTAN, Comte J. DE, Recherches sur quelques effluves terrestres [Researches on some terrestrial emanations], Paris.

38 THE DIVINING ROD.

1827. FRORIEP, L. VON, Notizèn aus dem Gebiete der Natur- und Heilkunde, Erfurt. See vol. 17, No. 1 (No. 353), pp. 1-9.

1833. CHEVREUL, M. E., Lettre à M. Ampère sur une classe particulière de mouvemens musculaires [Letter to Mr. Ampère on a certain class of muscular movements. An article on the divining rod and the magic pendulum]. Revue des deux-mondes, vol. 2, pp. 248-257.

1835. GRIMM, JACOB, Deutsche Mythologie [German mythology], Göttingen. 2d ed. [Etymology of Wünschelrute], pp. 926-928, 1854.

1836-1842. GORRES, JOSEPH VON, Die christliche Mystik [The Christian mystic], vols., Regensburg and Landshut. See vol. 3, pp. 186, 208.

1837. GILARDIN, ALPHONSE, Un procès à Lyon en 1692, ou Aymar, l'homme à la baguette [A trial at Lyon in 1692, or Aymar, the man of the divining rod]. Revue du Lyonnais, vol. 5, pp. 81-99.

1840. MENESTRIER, CL.-FR., Réflexions sur les indications de la baguette [Reflections on the indications of the divining rod], Lyons, 1694; reprinted under the title De la baguette divinatoire, at Avignon.

1843. GRASSE, JOH. G. TH., Bibliotheca magica et pneumatica [Library of magic and spiritism], Leipzig.

1844. LOUBERT, J. B., Le magnétisme et le somnambulisme devant les corps des savants, la cour de Rome et les théologiens [Magnetism and somnambulism before the scholars, the court of Rome, and the theologians], published anonymously, Paris.

1845. YSABEAU, A., Hydroscopie, L'Abbé Paramelle [Hydroscopy, Abbé Paramelle]: Journal d'agriculture pratique et de jardinage, publié * * * sous la direction de Alex. Bixio, 2d ser., vol. 2, pp. 456-460, Paris.

1846. FORNARI. See Giraldo, M. de.

1846. GIRALDO, M. DE, Histoire curieuse et pittoresque des sorciers, devins, magiciens, astrologues, voyants, revenants, etc., depuis l'antiquité jusqu'à nos jours. Revue et augmentée par M. Fornari [Curious and picturesque history of sorcerers, diviners, magicians, astrologers, clairvoyants, spirit mediums, etc., from antiquity to the present time. Reviewed and enlarged by Mr. Fornari], pp. 124-125, Paris.

1846. LATOUR, BENOÎT, Le véritable assureur des récoltes [The true guarantor of crops]. Journal des engrais, February, Orleans.

1846-47. DALLAC, Abbé, Faut-il croire à la baguette? [Is it necessary to believe in the divining rod?]: Soc. des lettres, sci. et arts l'Aveyron Mém., vol. 6.

1847. DEGOUSÉE, J., Guide du sondeur [Guide to the driller], Paris.

1848. CHEVALIER, Abbé CASIMIR, La baguette divinatoire justifiée scientifiquement [The divining rod scientifically justified], Tours. 2d ed., 1853.

1848. MEYER, CARL, Der Aberglaube des Mittelälters und der nächstfolgenden Jahrhunderte [The superstition of the Middle Ages and following centuries], Basel. 8+382 pp.

1848. MIGNE, Abbé [Jacques Albien Simon Collin, known as Collin de Plancy], Dictionnaire des sciences occultes [Dictionary of occult sciences], 2 vols., Paris. Baguette divinatoire [The divining rod], vol. 1, pp. 162-172.

1849. La clef des sources ou l'art de les découvrir [The key to springs or the art of discovering them], par un ecclésiastique du diocèse de Langres, Langres.

1849. MORTILLET, GABRIEL, Histoire de l'hydroscopie et de la baguette divinatoire [History of hydroscopy and of the divining rod], Chambery.

1849. NORK, F., Die Sitten und Gebräuche der Deutschen und ihrer Nachbarvölker [The customs and usages of Germans and their neighbors], Stuttgart.

1850-1852. SAINTE-TULLE, LAZARE DE, articles in L'érudition, vols. 1 and 2, Versailles.

1851. COLQUHOUN, J. C., An history of magic, witchcraft, and animal magnetism, 2 vols., London. See vol. 2, pp. 254–284.

1851. JACQUET, Abbé, Solution du problème concernant l'origine et la découverte des sources [Solution of the problem of the origin and the discovery of springs], Lyons.

1851. MAYO, HERBERT, On the truths contained in popular superstitions, with an account of mesmerism, Edinburgh and London, 2d ed.

1851. Solutions de problèmes concernant l'origine et la découverte des sources, ou entretiens d'un chevalier révélant à son fils la découverte des principes hydrogéologiques [Solution of problems concerning the origin and discovery of springs, or conversations of a knight revealing to his son the discovery of hydrogeologic principles], Lyons.

1853. BERSOT, ERNEST, Mesmer et le magnétisme animal [Mesmer and animal magnetism], Paris. See pp. 121–132.

1853. PHIPPEN, F., Narrative of practical experiments proving to demonstrate the discovery of water, coal, and minerals in the earth by means of the dowsing fork or divining rod, London.

1853. RIONDET, D'HYÈRES, La baguette divinatoire employée à la recherche des eaux souterraines [The divining rod employed in finding underground waters]: Memoir presented before the Academy of Sciences of Paris.

1853. SCHMIDT, C. W., Zur Rhabdomantie, den Erscheinungen mit der Wünschelrute gehörig [On rhabdomancy, the phenomena peculiar to the divining rod]: Magikon, vol. 5, p. 106, Stuttgart.

1854. CARUS, C. G., Lebensmagnetismus-Magie [Vital magnetism magic]: Die Gegenwart, vol. 10, Berlin.

1854. CHEVREUL, M. E., De la baguette divinatoire, du pendule dit explorateur, et des tables tournantes, au point de vue de l'histoire, de la critique et de la méthode expérimentale [On the divining rod, the so-called exploring pendulum, and turning tables, from the point of view of history, criticism, and the experimental method], Paris.

1854. MOROGUES, BARON DE, Observations sur le fluide organo-électrique et sur les mouvements électrométriques des baguettes et des pendules [Observations on the organo-electric fluid and on the electrometric movements of divining rods and magic pendulums], Paris.

1854–55. REICHENBACH, KARL L. F. VON, Der sensitive Mensch und sein Verhalten zum Od [The sensitive man and his relation to od], 2 vols., Stuttgart.

1856. COTTA, BERNHARD, Quellenkunde: Lehre von der Bildung und Auffindung der Quellen [Springs: Information on the formation and discovery of springs], as an introduction to L'art de découvrir les sources, by Abbé Paramelle, Leipzig, 1856; Paris, 1859.

1856. DUMAS, J., La science des fontaines, ou moyen sûr et facile de créer partout des sources d'eau potable [The science of springs, or sure and easy means of establishing everywhere springs of potable water], 1856; new ed., 1857, contains a chapter on the divining rod (pp. 251–256).

1856. GAETZSCHMANN, MORIZ FERDINAND, Die Auf- und Untersuchung von Lagerstätten nutzbarer Mineralien [The discovery and investigation of deposits of useful minerals], Freiberg. See pp. 293–308.

1856. PARAMELLE, Abbé, L'art de découvrir les sources [The art of finding springs], 5 editions, from 1856 to 1907.

1857. RÉSIE, Comte de, Histoire et traité des sciences occultes * * * [History and treatise on occult sciences * * *], 2 vols., Paris. See vol. 2, ch. 5, pp. 159–177.

1858. Biot, J. B., Mélanges scientifiques et littéraires [Scientific and literary miscellany], 3 vols., Paris. See pp. 72-77 of the chapter on charlatanism in vol. 2.
1858. Jacob, P. L. [P. Lacroix], Curiosités des sciences occultes [Curiosities of the occult sciences], Paris. Baguette divinatoire (divining rod) under "Alchimie," on pp. 141-155 of edition of 1862.
1858. Lacroix, P. See Jacob, P. L.
1860. Figuier, Louis, Les mystères de la science [The mysteries of science], 1860.
1860-61. Figuier, Louis, Histoire du merveilleux dans les temps modernes [History of the marvelous in modern times], 4 vols., Paris. See vol. 2, pp. 1-175.
1861. Amy, F., de Pennessières (Jura), Voyages d'un hydroscope, ou l'art de découvrir les sources [Journeys of a hydroscope, or the art of discovering springs], Paris.
1861. Jacquet, Abbé, De l'hydrogéologie [On hydrology—origin and discovery of springs], new ed., Lyons.
1861. Richard, Abbé Pierre, article in L'indépendant de Saintes, Mar. 14.
1862. Dufour, La baguette divinatoire [The divining rod]: Revue savoisienne, 3d year, p. 34, Annecy.
1862. Descosse, de Forcalquier, La découverte des sources et exploration des eaux souterraines [The discovery of springs and the exploration of underground waters], Marseilles. New ed., 1883.
1862. Krause, Ernst. See Sterne, Carus.
1862. Sterne, Carus (Ernst Krause), Die Wahrsagung aus den Bewegungen lebloser Körper unter dem Einflusse der menschlichen Hand [Divination by the movements of lifeless bodies under the influence of the human hand], Weimar.
1863-64. Bizouard, Jos., Des rapports de l'homme avec le démon [Some relations between man and the devil], 6 vols., Paris. See vols. 2 and 3.
1863. Carrié, Abbé, L'hydroscopographie et métalloscopographie, ou l'art de découvrir les sources et les gisements métallifères au moyen de l'électro-magnétisme [Hydroscopy and metalloscopy, or the art of discovering springs and metalliferous deposits by means of electromagnetism], Saintes.
1863. Peretti, A., Delle serate del villagio [Evenings in the village], Ivree. No. 4, The divining rod.
1865. Emsmann, H., Die Wünschelrute [The divining rod]: Westerm. illustr. deutsch. Monatsh., vol. 18, Brunswick.
1866. Baring-Gould, S., Curious myths of the Middle Ages, London. New impression, London, New York, etc., pp. 55-92, 1901.
1870. Romain, Manuel du sondeur-puisatier-hydroscope [Manual for the driller, well borer, hydroscopist].
1873. Fiske, John, Myths and myth-makers, Cambridge, Mass.
1873. Nöggerath, Jacob, Beiträge zur Geschichte der Bergknappen [Contributions to the history of miners]: Zeitschr. Bergrecht, 14th year, Bonn.
1876. Latimer, Charles, The divining rod: virgula divina baculus divinatoribus, water witching, Cleveland.
1876. Nöggerath, Jacob, Die Berggeister und die Glücks- oder Wünschelruthe in alteren Zeiten besonders bei den Bergleuten [The mountain sprites and the divining rod in olden times, especially among miners]: Westermann's Jahrbuch, Braunschweig, pp. 182-188.
1876-1879. Laforet, Aug., Le bâton, étude historique et littéraire [The wand, a historical and literary study], 2 vols., Marseilles. See vol. 1, ch. 9, pp. 248-281.
1878. Haslinger, Camillo, Das Quellensuchen [Spring finding]: Psychische Studien, 5th year, November, pp. 483-486, Leipzig.

1879. CLAVAIROZ, M. F. (Léon Favre), Die Wünschelrute [The divining rod]: Psychische Studien, 6th year, July, Leipzig.

1879. FAVRE, LÉON. *See* Clavairoz, M. F.

1879. FONVIELLE, W. DE, Comment se font les miracles en-déhors de l'église [How miracles occur without the church], Paris, no date (about 1879). New edition under the title: Les saltimbanques de la science. Comment ils font les miracles [The humbugs of science. How miracles happen], Paris, no date.

1882. CAUDÉRAN, HIPPOLYTE, Découverte des sources. Notice scientifique sur l'abbé Richard et l'hydroscopie [Discovery of springs. Scientific note on Abbé Richard and hydroscopy], Bordeaux.

1882. KÖHLER, G., article in Glückauf, Schneeberg.

1882. LAFFINEUR, JULES, Hydraulique et hydrologie souterraine et superficielle, ou traité de la science des sources, de la création des fontaines, de la captation et de l'aménagement des eaux pour tous les besoins agricoles et industriels [Hydraulics and underground and surficial hydrology, or a treatise on the science of springs, the formation of fountains, the acquisition and management of water supplies for all agricultural and industrial needs], Paris.

1883. HELLAND, A., Om ønskelvisten [On the divining rod]: Dagbladet, No. 151, June 11, Christiania.

1883. LANG, ANDREW, The divining rod: Cornhill Magazine, vol. 47, pp. 83–91, London.

1883. LOCHMANN, Prof., discussion in Dagbladet, No. 153, June 13, Christiania.

1883. RAYMOND, R. W., The divining rod: Am. Inst. Min. Eng. Trans., vol. 11; and U. S. Geol. Survey Mineral Resources, 1882, pp. 610–626, 1883.

1884. LANG, ANDREW, Custom and myth, London. 2d ed., pp. 180–196, 1885.

1884. PEASE, EDW. R., The divining rod: Soc. Psychical Research Proc., vol. 2, pp. 78–107, London.

1884. STINDE, JULIUS, Das Geheimnis der Wünschelrute [The secret of the divining rod]: Schorers Familienblatt, 5 vols., pp. 649–650, 682–683, Berlin.

1885. JACOB, P. L. [P. Lacroix], Curiosités des sciences occultes [Curiosities of the occult sciences], Paris.

1886. HAUSSEN, J. S. (K. Kiesewetter), Zur Geschichte der Bewegungsphänomene [On the history of motion phenomena]: Sphinx, vol. 2, pp. 115–129, Gera.

1886. MEUNIER, Mme. STANISLAS, Les sources [Springs]: Biblioth. des merveilles, No. 3, Paris.

1886. PEASE, EDW., Die Wünschelrute [The divining rod]: Sphinx, vol. 2, pp. 69–78, Gera.

1886. ROCHAS, ALBERT DE, La polarité vitale [Vital polarity]: Cosmos, new ser., Apr. 19, vol. 4, pp. 59–63.

1887. BONNEMÈRE [LIONEL], La baguette des sourciers vendéens [The rod of Vendean sorcerers]: Soc. d'anthrop. Paris Bull., vol. 10, pp. 780–782.

1890. KUHLENBECK, LUDWIG, Spaziergänge eines Wahrheitssuchers ins Reich der Mystik [Walks of a truth seeker in the realm of the mystic], Leipzig. See ch. 11, pp. 165–172.

1891. KIESEWETTER, CARL, Geschichte des neueren Occultismus [History of the new occultism], Leipzig. See pp. 512–539.

1892. SCHWARTZ, WILHELM, Die Wünschelrute als Quellen- und Schatzsucher [The divining rod as a spring and treasure searcher]: Ver. Volkskunde Zeitschr., 2d year, pp. 67–78, Berlin.

1893. BJERGE, PAUL. *See* Feilberg, H. F.

1893. FEILBERG, H. F., Spåstikken [The divining rod], in Aarbog for Dansk Kultur historie [Yearbook for Danish culture history], by Paul Bjerge, Aarhus.

1893. MULLINS, JOHN, The divining rod; its history, truthfulness, and practical utility, Corsham, Wiltshire.

1893. PREL, KARL DU, Die Wünschelrute [The divining rod]: Die Zukunft, vol. 4, pp. 215-225, Berlin.

1895. HAAS, H. J., Quellenkunde, Lehre von der Bildung und vom Vorkommen der Quellen und des Grundwassers [Springs. Information on the formation and occurrence of springs and ground water], pp. 184-196, Leipzig.

1896. OSTWALD, WILHELM, Elektrochemie, ihre Geschichte und Lehre [Electrochemistry, its history and doctrine], ch. 8, p. 230, Leipzig.

1897. BARRETT, W. F., The divining rod, Nature, vol. 56, pp. 568-569, London.

1897. CHALON, P., Sur la recherche des eaux souterraines [On the investigation of ground water]: Soc. ingénieurs civils de France, Mém., vol. 2, pp. 38-39, Paris.

1897. HOLMES, T. V., On the evidence for the efficacy of the diviner and his rod in the search for water: Anthropol. Inst. of Great Britain and Ireland Jour., vol. 27, pp. 233-259, London.

1897-1900. BARRETT, W. F., On the so-called divining rod or virgula divina: Soc. Psychical Res. Proc. (London), vol. 13, 1897, and vol. 15, pp. 130-383, 1900.

1898. BONNIOT, CHANOINE V. DE, [letter on the discovery of water by means of the magic pendulum]: Revue du monde invisible, Oct. 15, p. 314.

1898. BROTHIER DE ROLLIÈRE. [See Gué, P. du, and Brothier de Rollière.

1898. GUÉ, P. DU, and BROTHIER DE ROLLIÈRE, [article on Thouvenel]: L'intermédiaire des chercheurs et des curieux, vol. 37, pp. 226, 732-733, Paris.

1898-99. MORINAIS, G. DE LA, Les sourciers sont-ils sorciers? [Are the water witches sorcerers?]: Revue du monde invisible, 1st year, No. 2, pp. 88-92, Paris.

1898. LEHMANN, ALFRED, Aberglaube und Zauberei von den ältesten Zeiten an bis in die Gegenwart [Superstition and magic from the earliest times to the present], pp. 201-203, 375-377, 480, Stuttgart,.

1898. PARVILLE, HENRI DE, [two articles on water witching]: Le correspondant, Jan. 10, pp. 170-178, and Feb. 10, pp. 585-590.

1898. TARDIVEL, J. B., La baguette divinatoire et les sourciers [The divining rod and the water witches]: Revue du monde invisible, Paris, Sept. 15, pp. 231-233.

1899. AUSCHER, E. S., L'art de découvrir les sources et de les capter [The art of discovering and developing underground waters]: Bibliothèque des connaissances utiles, vol. 49, 1st ed., Paris. 2d ed., 1905.

1899. BEAVEN, E. W., Tales of the divining rod, London.

1899. PREL, KARL DU, Die Magie als Naturwissenschaft [Magic as a natural science], 2 vols., Jena.

1899. VERNHES, Abbé A., Les sourciers ne sont pas des sorciers [Water witches are not sorcerers]: Revue du monde invisible, July 15.

1900. ARDOUANE, paper in L'Intermédiaire des chercheurs et des curieux, vol. 41, col. 451.

1900. BEAUCORPS, A. ET F. DE, Étude empirique, au moyen de la baguette, sur les origines souterraines de la rivière du Loiret. Projet de captation d'eau pour la ville de Paris. Historique de la baguette divinatoire, théorie de son emploi, application au val de la Loire et aux sources du Loiret [Empirical study, by means of the divining rod, of the underground source of the river of the Loiret. Project for obtaining water for the city of Paris. History of the divining rod, theory of its use, application to the valley of the Loire and to the springs of the Loiret], Orleans.

1900. GUÉ, P. DU, and BROTHIER DE ROLLIÈRE, articles in L'intermédiaire des chercheurs et des curieux, vol. 42, pp. 162-163, 409-410, Paris.

1900. DELANNE, GABRIEL, D'où vient le pouvoir des sourciers? [Whence comes the ability of water witches?]: Jour. du magnétisme et de la psychologie, 55th year, Paris.

1900. DURVILLE, H. (director Soc. magnétique en France), Jour. du magnétisme et de la psychologie, No. 1, January, and following numbers.

1900. GATAKER, L., alias ISMALA, Un sourcier moderne [A modern water witch]: Jour. du magnétisme et de la psychologie, No. 6, June, Paris.

1900. ISMALA. See Gataker, L.

1900. COUSSIÈRE, LA, article in L'intermédiaire des chercheurs et des curieux, 36th year, vol. 41, col. 283, Paris.

1900. MARTELLIÈRE, [On the divining rod]: L'intermédiaire des chercheurs et des curieux, 36th year, vol. 41, col. 305, Paris.

1901. GAST, A., Un sourcier [A water witch]: Moniteur des études psychiques, 25th year, No. 3, Feb. 5, Paris.

1901. SAINT-CLOUD, P., Un homme étrange [A strange man]: Moniteur des études psychiques, 25th year, Paris.

1902. BATTANDIER, A., Sur la baguette divinatoire [On the divining rod]: Cosmos, May; Revue du monde invisible, Nov. 15.

1902. LEFEBRE, A., article in Cosmos, June 14, Paris.

1902. URBAN, MICHAEL, Wünschelruthe, Wunschspiegel und Zauberwurzeln [Divining rod, magic mirror, and magic roots]: Mittheil. Nordböhm. Excursions-Clubs, pp. 350–357, Leipa.

1903. BEYSCHLAG, F., Aus dem wissenschaftlichen Leben * * * der Wünschelrute [From the scientific life * * * the divining rod]: Naturwiss. Wochenschr., vol. 18, pp. 321–322, Apr. 5.

1903. BOURCARD, I. I., Zur Frage der Wünschelruthe [On the question of the divining rod]: Psychische Studien, 30th year, pp. 212–213, Leipzig.

1903. BÜLOW-BOTHKAMP, CAI VON, [Personal experiments in rhabdomancy]: Prometheus, 14th year, No. 687, pp. 173–174, Berlin. Partisan.

1903. DARAPSKY, L., Altes und Neues von der Wünschelrute [Old and new ideas on the divining rod], Leipzig.

1903–4. DIÉNERT, F., Contribution à l'étude des courants souterrains au moyen de la boussole et des courants électro-magnétiques [Contribution to the study of underground currents by means of the compass and electro-magnetic currents]: Soc. belge de la géologie et d'hydrologie Mém.

1903. FALKENHORST, C., Alte und moderne Wünschelrutenforscher [Ancient and modern divining-rod investigators]: Die Gartenlaube, Leipzig.

1903. FAUCHON, Dr., Rapport sur le mémoire qui précède—Les fluides bacillogires étudiés au moyen de la furcelle par de Comte de Tristan [Report on the preceding memoir. The bacillogic fluids studied by means of the forked stick by Count Tristan]: Soc. agr., sci., belles lettres et arts d'Orléans Mém., vol. 3, pp. 322–336.

1903. GRASSET, Dr., L'hypnotisme et la suggestion [Hypnotism and suggestion].

1903. GAGEL, C., Das Grundwasser [Ground water]: Naturwiss. Wochenschr., No. 30, Apr. 26.

1903. GAGEL, C., Der "Nutzen" der Wünschelrute [The "use" of the divining rod]: Prometheus, No. 69, pp. 353–356, Berlin.

1903. HIRSCHFELD, LUDWIG, Internationale Mineralquellen-Zeitung, Vienna.

1903. KEILHACK, K., article in Naturwiss. Wochenschr., No. 27, vol. 18, pp. 321–322, Apr. 5, Jena.

1903. KNIEPP, A., Zum Problem der Wünschelrute [On the divining-rod problem]: Psychische Studien, 30th year, pp. 82–89, Leipzig.

1903. LANGE, G. A., article in Die übersinnliche Welt, 11th year, p. 107, Berlin.
1903. LEPPLA, A., article in Naturwiss. Wochenschr., 18th year, pp. 321–322, Jena.
1903. NAGEL, L., article in Die übersinnliche Welt, 11th year, pp. 107, 192, 435, Berlin.
1903. RICHTER, EMIL, Die Wünschelrute [The divining rod]: Sächsische Volkskunde Mitteil., Dresden.
1903. SÖKELAND, HERMANN, Die Wünschelrute [The divining rod]: Ver. Volkskunde Zeitschr., 13th year, pt. 2, pp. 34–43, Berlin.
1903. Sourciers * * * sorciers? Peut-on voir l'eau sous terre? [Water witches * * * sorcerers? Can one see water under the ground?]: Les lectures pour tous, 5th year, August.
1903. SURBLED, GEORGES, Le secret des sourciers [The secret of water witches], Paris, 1st ed., 1903; 2d ed., 1908.
1903. TRISTAN, Comte J. de, Les fluides bacillogires étudiés au moyen de la furcelle [Bacillogic fluids studied by means of the furcelle]: Soc. d'agr., sci., belles lettres et arts d'Orléans Mém., vol. 3, pp. 280–336, Orleans.
1903. UHL, G., Die Wünschelrute [The divining rod]: Daheim, Berlin, Sept. 12, pp. 18–21.
1904. CHABRAND, ERNEST, La baguette divinatoire et les sourciers. Les phénomènes de la baguette. Le Bletonisme. Les faits et les théories [The divining rod and diviners. The phenomena of the divining rod. Bletonism. Facts and theories]: Soc. dauphin. d'ethnol. et d'anthropol. Bull., vol. 2, Grenoble.
1904. GRASSET, Dr., Le spiritisme devant la science [Spiritualism in the presence of science]: Montpellier and Paris.
1904. HENNIG, RICH., Wunder und Wissenschaft; eine Kritik und Erklärung der okkulten Phänomene [Wonder and science; a criticism and elucidation of occult phenomena], Hamburg.
1904. KLAPPER, J., Beschwörungsformeln bei Gewinnung der Wünschelrute [Formulae of exorcism for use in obtaining the divining rod]: Schlesischen Gesell. Volkskunde Mitteil., vol. 6, pt. 14, pp. 51–58, Breslau.
1904. PABST, CAMILLE, Recherche et captage des eaux souterraines [The investigation and acquisition of ground waters]: L'agriculture moderne, supplement agricole du Petit journal, 9th year, Paris.
1904. POETTERS, KARL, Die Wünschelruthe [The divining rod]: Brandeburgia, 12th year, Berlin.
1905. DIEFENBACH, M., article in Die Umschau, No. 37, p. 740.
1905–6. EHLERT, H., article in Technisches Gemeindeblatt, No. 19, p. 296, Berlin.
1905. EHLERT, H., Zur Wünschelruthenfrage [On the divining-rod question]: Zentralbl. Bauverwaltung, Nos. 103 and 104, Berlin.
1905. FRANZIUS, G., Die Wünschelrute [The divining rod]: Deutsche Klempner-Zeitung, 25th year, Berlin, and Zentralbl. Bauverwaltung, 25th year, No. 74, pp. 461–462, Berlin.
1905. GRASSET, Dr., article in Revue des deux-mondes, Mar. 15.
1905. HEIM, A., Das Quellenfinden mit der Wünschelrute [Spring finding with the divining rod]: Zeitschr. Bayer. Rev., 9th year, Munich. In 1907 Mr. Heim called a conference of the Society of Sciences of Zurich to discuss rhabdomancy.
1905. HILDEBRANDT, GOTTHOLD, Zum Problem der Wünschelrute [On the problem of the divining rod]: Das Echo, 24th year, June 22, pp. 1971–1974, Berlin.
1905. SCHMIDT, E., article in Deutsche Welt, 8th year, Nov. 5, Berlin.
1905. WEBER, L., Die Wünschelrute [The divining rod], Kiel and Leipsic.

1906. ARÚDY, L. D', La baguette magique [The magic wand]: L'écho du merveilleux, No. 236, pp. 412–413, Paris.

1906. BAVIR, H., Über die wahrscheinliche Möglichkeit der Aufsuchung von nutzbaren Erzlagerstätten mittelst einer photographischen Aufnahme ihrer elektrischen Ausstrahlung [On the apparent possibility of discovering useful ore deposits by photographing their electric emanations], Prague.

1906-7. BERGER, Die Wünschelrute und zur Wünschelrutenfrage [The divining rod and on the divining-rod question]: Der Kulturtechniker, 9th and 10th years, Breslau.

1906. BIRK, A., articles in Neue Freie Presse, Aug. 30, Vienna.

1906. DESSOIR, MAX, Die Wünschelrute [The divining rod]: Die Woche, No. 38, pp. 1637–1639, Berlin.

1906. DRYVER, F. W., Mozaïek allerlei op het gebied van geschiedenis, volkseigenaardigheded, etc. [Miscellaneous gleanings in history, popular customs, etc.], Groningen.

1906. EHLERT, H., Wider die Wünschelrute [Against the divining rod]: Schillings Jour. Gasbeleuchtung und Wasserversorgung, 49th year, pp. 71–75, 402–404, Berlin.

1906. ERBSTEIN, A., Die Wünschelrute [The divining rod]: Illustr. Zeitung, vol. 120, Leipzig.

1906. FÜRSTENAU, R., Theorien und Experimente über die Wünschelrute [Theories and experiments on the divining rod]: Die Umschau, No. 38, Frankfurt, 1906; see also Technische Rundschau, Nos. 16 and 17, April, 1909.

1906. GESSMANN, G., article in Arena, No. 6, pp. 617–622, Berlin.

1906. GRASSET, Dr., Le psychisme inférieur [The inferior psychics], Paris.

1906. HEINRICHS, LUDW., Die Wünschelrute [The divining rod]: Die Wahrheit, 40th year, pp. 727–734, Munich and Stuttgart.

1906. HOPPE, O., Die Wünschelrute, der Franklin'sche Blitzableiter und die Antenne der drahtlosen Telegraphie in technisch-wissenschaftlichem Zusammenhange [The divining rod, the Franklin lightning rod, and the antennae of the wireless telegraph in technical relationship]: Naturwiss. Wochenschr., 21st year, pp. 609–616, Jena.

1906. KNIEFF, ALBERT, Radioactivität und Wünschelruthe [Radioactivity and the divining rod]: Die Gegenwart, vol. 70, pp. 166–169, 182–184, Berlin.

1906. KULLMANN, HEINRICH, article in Schillings Jour. Gasbeleuchtung und Wasserversorgung, p. 75, Munich and Berlin.

1906. LA BAUME, W., Die Wünschelrute [The divining rod]: Kosmos, 3d year, pp. 201–205, 311, Stuttgart.

1906. LENÔTRE, G. articles in Le Monde illustré, Mar. 31; La nature, Apr. 15; L'Écho du merveilleux, Apr. 15.

1906. MAIER, F., Zur Erklärung der Wünschelrute [The explanation of the divining rod]: Psychische Studien, 33d year, pp. 550–554, Leipsic.

1906. MONTENAY DU MENHY, Comte de, Notes sur les sourciers [Notes on water witches]: L'écho du merveilleux, Paris, Sept. 1.

1906. OHNSTEIN, ALBERT, Ein automatischer Quellenfinder [An automatic spring finder (the Schmid apparatus)]: Technische Rundschau, 12th year, No. 47, pp. 613–614.

1906. REGE, EUGENON VON, Die Wünschelrute [The divining rod]: Der Deutsche, Sept. 29, Berlin.

1906. SIEGERT, A., Das Quellensuchen mit der Wünschelrute [Spring finding with the divining rod]: Zeitschr. Bayer. revis., 10th year, Munich.

1906. STOSS: P., [On the divining rod]: Die Übersinnliche Welt, 14th year, pp. 4, 57, 93, Berlin,

1906. TANCK, W., Die Wünschelrute [The divining rod]: Die Heimat, 16th year, Kiel.

1906. VIGEN, CHARLES, L'Abbé Richard, hydrogéologue: Étude sur sa vie et son secret pour la découverte des sources. L'hydroscopie sensitive et la baguette [The Abbé Richard, hydrogeologist: Study of his life and his secret for finding springs. Sensitive hydroscopy and the divining rod]: Revue de Saintonge, La Rochelle.

1906. VIGEN, CHARLES, La baguette divinatoire des sourciers [The divining rod of the water witches]: La nature, pp. 101–103.

1906. WARCOLIER, R., and BARRETT, W. F., [Experiments with the divining rod]: Annales des sci. psychiques, 16th year, pp. 745–751, Paris.

1906. WEISSENBERG, H., [Against the divining rod]: Die Umschau, No. 34, p. 680, Frankfort on the Main.

1906-7. WILLFORT, M., Das Wasserfinden mit der Wünschelrute [Water finding with the divining rod]: Bautechniker, 26th and 27th years, Vienna.

1906. WOLFF, WILHELM, [Against the divining rod]: Schillings Jour. Gasbeleuchtung und Wasserversorgung, Munich and Berlin.

1907. BIANCO, F., article in Le Corriere della sera, Apr. 9. Discusses the divining rod in Italy.

1907. BLOM, V., Zur Theorie der Wünschelrute [The theory of the divining rod]: Prometheus, 18th year, pp. 129–134, Berlin.

1907. DIENERT, FRÉDÉRIC, Hydrologie agricole [Agricultural hydrology]: Encyclopédie agricole, pp. 198–293, Paris.

1907. FIEBELKORN, Dr., Empfiehlt sich für den Ziegeleibesitzer die Anwendung der Wünschelrute zur Aufsuchung von Wasser auf seinem Grundstücke? [Is the use of the divining rod suitable for finding water on a brickyard owner's land?]: Deutsch..Ver. Ton-, Zement- und Kalkindustrie, Mitteil. Berlin.

1907. FITZ, J., Od und die Wünschelrute [Od and the divining rod]: Organ des "Verein der Bohrtechniker," 25th year, No. 9, pp. 103–106, Vienna; also Ver. Österr. Gesundheitstechniker Zeitschr., Vienna.

1907. FLEISCHMANN, Dr. O., Elektrische Metallfunde [Electrical metal finding]: Der Deutsche, June, pp. 409–411, Berlin.

1907. FRANZIUS, G., Meine Beobachtungen mit der Wünschelrute [My observations with the divining rod], Berlin.

1907. FRIEDRICH, ALBRECHT, Zur Erklärung der Wünschelrute [On the explanation of the divining rod]: Der Deutsche, August, pp. 582–584, Berlin.

1907. GOCKEL, A., Grundwasser und atmosphärische Elektrizität. Ein Beitrag zur Wünschelrutenfrage [Ground water and atmospheric electricity. A contribution to the divining-rod question]: Natur und Offenbarung, vol. 53, Münster.

1907. GOUPIL, Discussion en Allemagne sur la baguette divinatoire employée à découvrir les sources [Discussion in Germany on the divining rod employed to discover springs]: Annales des ponts et chaussées, 77th year, 8th ser., vol. 25, pp. 218–224, Paris.

1907. HELBIG, Die Wünschelrute [The divining rod]: Pharmazeut. Zentralhalle f. Deutschland, 48th year, pp. 185–189, 226–230, Dresden.

1907. HÜSING, G., Um die Wünschelrute [Concerning the divining rod], Dissen near Osnabruck.

1907. JAEGER, G., Nochmals die Wünschelrute [Once again the divining rod]: Prof. Dr. G. Jaeger's Monatsblatt, 26th year, pp. 33–36, 49–53, 67–69, Stuttgart.

1907. KNIEPF, A., Die Physik der Wünschelrute [The physics of the divining rod]: Zentralbl. f. Okkultismus, 1st year, pp. 9–12, Leipsic.

1907. KÖLLER-CAROW, VON, Das Fiasko der Wünschelrute [The failure of the divining rod]: Zeitschr. für Spiritusindustrie, 30th year, No. 8, p. 77, Berlin.

1907. KÖNIG, F., Ernstes und Heiteres aus dem Zauberreiche der Wünschelrute [Serious and comical from the fairy realm of the divining rod], Leipzig.

1907. OHLSEN, O., Die Wünschelrute in Italien [The divining rod in Italy]: Psychische Studien, 34th year, pp. 376–379, Leipzig.

1907. SCHOWALTER, A., Die Wünschelrute in Südafrica [The divining rod in South Africa]: Der Deutsche, Berlin.

1907. TRÉBUCQ, S., article in Jour. du magnétisme, vol. 33, 3e trimestre, Paris.

1907. VOGDT, Gegen die Wünschelrute [Against the divining rod]: Zeitschr. Spiritusindustrie, 30th year, No. 5, pp. 39–40, Berlin.

1907. VOGEL, P., Grenzfeststellungen mit der Wünschelrute [Establishing boundaries with the divining rod]: Zeitschr. Vermessungswesen, vol. 36, pp. 554–559, Stuttgart.

1907. WAPPLER, A. F., Alte sächsische Wünschelrutengeschichten [Old Saxon divining-rod stories]: Mitteil. d. Freiberger Altertums-Vereins, Freiberg.

1907. WOLFF, W., Wider die Wünschelrute [Against the divining rod]: Deutschen Ver. von Gas- und Wasserfachmänner Verh., Munich.

1908. DIENERT, F., A. GUILLERD, and MARREC, De l'emploi de l'acoustèle de Daguin pour la recherche des bruits souterrains [The use of the "acoustèle" of Daguin for the discovery of subterranean sounds]: Acad. sci. Comp. rend., vol. 146, pp. 1182–1184, Paris.

1908. HAUSSMANN, KARL, Die Wünschelrute und Ähnliches [The divining rod and similar devices]: Mitteil. aus dem Markscheiderwesen, pp. 74–78, Freiberg, Saxony.

1908. MÉRY, GASTON, Comment je me suis révélé sourcier [How I discovered myself to be a water witch]: L'écho du merveilleux, November; several other articles in the same journal, 1906–1908.

1908. SCHOBER, G., and REDLIEN, Aufruf gegen die Wünschelrute [Summons against the divining rod]: Pumpen- und Brunnenbau, 4th year, Berlin.

1908-9. SURYA, G. W., Die okkulte Seite der Wünschelrute [The occult side of the divining rod]: Zentralbl. für Okkultismus, 2d year, September, pp. 97–102, Leipzig.

1909. ADOLF, H., articles in Ver. Gas- und Wasserfachmänner in Österreich-Ungarn Zeitschr. No. 6, Mar. 15, and No. 10, May 15.

1909. AIGNER, EDOUARD (of Munich), Die Wünschelrute [The divining rod]: Jour. Gasbeleuchtung und Wasserversorgung, 52d year, pp. 936–939, Munich and Berlin.

1909. BAYER, H. C., Mit der Wünschelrute, etc. [With the divining rod, etc.], Stuttgart.

1909. BRAIKOWICH, F., article in Ver. Gas- und Wasserfachmänner in Österreich-Ungarn Zeitschr., No. 10, May 15.

1909. BRUNO, E., La radioactivité des sources [The radioactivity of springs]: L'écho du Merveilleux, Apr. 1.

1909. DOMINIK, H., Die Wünschelrute [The divining rod]: März, 3d year, No. 13, pp. 18–23, Munich.

1909. DREHER, K., Die Wünschelrute von Podebrad in Böhmen [The divining rod of Podebrad in Bohemia]: Über Land und Meer, 51st year, Stuttgart.

1909. DUFOURG, FR., La découverte des sources et le magnetisme animal [The discovery of springs and animal magnetism]: L'écho du merveilleux, October and December.

1909. DÜNKELBERG, Prof. Dr., Die Erschürfung der Quellen [The discovery of springs]: Das Wasser, 5th year, No. 28, October, Halle.

1909. FRANZIUS, G., Zur Wünschelrutenfrage [On the divining-rod question]: Zentralbl. der Bauverwaltung, 29th year, pp. 201–203, Berlin.

1909. FRENZEL, PAUL, Für die Wassermutung durch hierzu geeignete sensitiv veranlagte Personen [For water finding by persons fitted therefor by virtue of an endowed sensitiveness]: Zeitschr. Vereines der Gas- und Wasserf. in Oesterr.-Ungarn, No. 9, May, Vienna.

1909. GALLEGO, E., Descubrimiento de aguas subterráneas. El invento del P. García Muñoz. [The discovery of underground waters. The invention of P. García Muñoz]: La energía eléctrica, vols. 11 and 13, Madrid, 1909 and 1911.

1909. GRIMM, J., Wünschelrutenaberglaube [Divining-rod superstition]: Es Werde Licht, March, pp. 185–187, Munich.

1909. HARTMANN, A., Wünschelrute rediviva [The divining rod restored]: Urania, 2d year, No. 11, pp. 164–166, Vienna.

1909. JACOBY, Ein Beitrag zur Lösung der Wünschelrutenfrage [A contribution to the solution of the divining-rod question]: Wochenschr. Architekt. zu Berlin, 4th year.

1909. MAGER, HENRI, Les radiations des corps minéraux; recherches des mines et des sources par leurs radiations [The radiations of mineral bodies; the search for mines and springs by their radiations], 3d ed., Paris.

1909. POSKIN, A., La rabdomancie ou l'art de découvrir les mines et les sources au moyen de la baguette divinatoire [Rhabdomancy, or the art of finding mines and springs by means of the divining rod]: Soc. belge. de géol., paléont. et hydrol. Mém., vol. 23, pp. 28–57. ·

1909. ROHRBACH, Dr. P., Wassererschliessung in Deutsch-Südwestafrika [Water finding in German Southwest Africa]: Kolonie und Heimat in Wort und Bild, 2d year, No. 14, pp. 2–3, Berlin.

1909. SCHMIDS, ADOLF, Automatischen Wasserfinder [Automatic water finder]: Deutsch. Landw. Mitteil., vol. 24, Berlin.

1909. WEGNER, Dr., [Against the divining rod]: Natur und Offenbarung, vol. 45, pp. 600–615, Münster i. W.

1910. BARRETT, W. F., The history and mystery of the so-called divining or dowsing rod, London.

1910. BIESKE, E., Für und wider die Wünschelrute [For and against the divining rod]: Jour. Gasbeleuchtung und Wasserversorgung, 53d year, pp. 885–896, Munich and Berlin.

1910. ENDRISS, KARL, Zum Problem der Wünschelrute [On the divining-rod problem]: Psychische Studien, 37th year, pp. 449–456, Leipzig.

1910. ENDRISS, KARL, Wünschelrute und Wasserfachmänner [The divining rod and professional water finders].

1910. GEINITZ, E., Experimente mit der Wünschelrute [Experiments with the divining rod]: Aus der Natur, 6th year, pp. 641–644, Leipzig.

1910. GUILLEMAIN, C., Die Wünschelrute [The divining rod]: Das Wasser, 6th year, pp. 223–224, Halle.

1910. HEYD, TH., Von der Wünschelrute und vom automatischen Quellenfinden [On the divining rod and automatic water finders]: D. Städt. Tiefbau, Heidelberg.

1910. HOCH, J., Die Wünschelrute [The divining rod]: Deutsch. landw. Gesell. Mitteil., vol. 25, Berlin.

1910. KLINCKOWSTROEM, Graf CARL VON, Virgula divina. Ein Beitrag zur Geschichte der Wünschelrute [Virgula divina. A contribution to the history of the divining rod]: Dokumente des Fortschritts, 4th year, pp. 583–588, Berlin.

1910. KNIEPF, ALBERT, Die Wünschelrute und die Wissenschaft [The divining rod and science]: Psychische Studien, 37th year, pp. 114–117, Leipzig.

1910. LANCELIN, CHARLES, La sorcellerie des campagnes [The witchcraft of the countryside], Paris.

1910. L'art des sourciers [The art of water witches]: Les inventions illustrées, 13th year, Paris.

1910. Les baguettes divinatoires métalliques et les procédés pseudo-scientifiques [Metallic divining rods and pseudo-scientific methods]: L'eau, March 15, Asnières near Paris.

1910. MAGER, HENRI, Un appareil scientifique pour la découverte des sources [A scientific apparatus for finding springs]: L'édilité technique, Paris.

1910. MAGER, HENRI, Pour découvrir les sources, les mines et les trésors au moyen de la baguette divinatoire et de divers appareils scientifiques [For the discovery of springs, mines, and treasures by means of the divining rod and various scientific apparatuses], 2d ed., Paris.

1910. MAGER, HENRI, Sur la baguette divinatoire pour la découverte des sources, mines et trésors [On the divining rod for the discovery of springs, mines, and treasures]: L'écho du merveilleux, Paris.

1910. MAGER, HENRI, Les radiations de la terre, et expériences susceptibles de prouver les causes des mouvements de certaines baguettes [The radiations of the earth, and experiments adapted to prove the causes of the movements of certain divining rods]: First Cong. Exper. Psychology Rept., pp. 196–206, November, Paris.

1910. METHA, H. K., Experiments with the water finder of Messrs. Mansfield & Co. in the trap area of western India: Dept. Agr. Bull. 38, Bombay.

1910. ROTHE, GEORG, Die Wünschelrute. Historisch-theoretische Studie [The divining rod. Historical-theoretical study], Jena.

1910. SLOET, L. A. J. W., De planten in het Germaansche volksgeloof en volksgebruik [Plants in Teutonic beliefs and customs], p. 80, 's Gravenhage.

1910. VOLL, Dr. ADAM, Die Wünschelrute und der siderische Pendel. Ein Versuch zu einer praktisch-wissenschaftlichen Studie [The divining rod and the sidereal pendulum. An attempt at a practical scientific study], Leipzig.

1910. WEBER, M., Prof. Weber über die Wünschelrute [Prof. Weber on the divining rod]: Das Wasser, 6th year, No. 28, pp. 578–579, Halle.

1910. WOLFF, W., Haben die geologischen Landesanstalten die Pflicht, gegen das Unwesen der Wünschelrute vorzugehen? [Is it the duty of geologic institutions to antagonize the divining-rod nuisance?]: Protokoll. ü. d. Versamml. d. Direkt. d. geolog. landes d. deutsch. Bundes-stat., Berlin.

1911. AIGNER, ED., Die Wünschelrute [The divining rod]: Balneol. Zeitschr., 22d year, Berlin.

1911. AIGNER, ED., Der gegenwärtige Stand der Wünschelruten-Forschung [The present status of divining-rod investigations], Munich. Published as a preface to the bibliography by Klinckowstroem.

1911. BARRETT, W. F., The so-called divining or dowsing rod: Psychical research [Home Library series], ch. 12, pp. 167–186, London.

1911. BEHME, Dr., Die Wünschelrute: zur Frage der Wasserbeschaffung [The divining rod; on the question of procuring water]: Illustr. Rundschau, 1st year, Hanover.

1911. BEYER, P., Ein Beitrag zur Klärung der Wünschelrutenfrage [A contribution for the elucidation of the divining-rod question]: Deutsche Briefzeit, 7th year, Naunhof near Leipzig.

1911. BORMANN, W., Allerhand über die Wünschelrute [Miscellaneous items on the divining rod]: Die übersinnliche Welt, 19th year, Berlin.

1911. BRAIKOWICH, F., Zur Wünschelrutenfrage [On the divining-rod question]: Ver. Gas- und Wasserfachmänner in Österreich-Ungarn Zeitschr., vol. 51, Vienna.

1911. BRUNNHOFER, H., Der Wünschelrutenwahn [The divining-rod mania]: Sonn-tagsblatt des "Bund" 1911, Berne.

1911. CARMEJEANNE, C., letters in L'eau, 1910, and in Jour. du magnétisme et du psychisme expér.

1911. DOBBERKAU, E. W., Experimente über Wasserfühlen von Quellen in der Erdentiefe [Experiments on the detection of water in underground springs]: Die übersinnliche Welt, 19th year, Berlin.

1911. DOUXAMI, HENRI, La rabdomancie ou l'art de la baguette divinatoire [Rhabdomancy, or the art of the divining rod]: Soc. linnéenne de Lyon Annales, vol. 57, pp. 33-49.

1911. DREYER, OTTO, Mythologische Deutung der Wünschelrute [Mythological significance of the divining rod]: Niedersachsen, 17th year, Bremen.

1911. FRANZIUS, G., Zur Wünschelrutenfrage [On the divining-rod question]: Ver. Gas- und Wasserf. in Österr.-Ungarn Zeitschr., vol. 51, Vienna.

1911. GERHARD, WILLIAM PAUL, Ein Beitrag zur Wünschelrutenfrage [A contribution to the divining-rod question]: Gesundheitsingenieur, 34th year, Munich and Berlin.

1911. GRAEVE, OTTO EDLER VON, Die Wünschelrute und ihre Anwendung in der Praxis [The divining rod and its application in practice], Osterode.

1911. HESSE, Dr., Altes and Neues von der Wünschelrute [The old and new of the divining rod]: Hygiene und Industrie, Dresden.

1911. HOHENFELS, HANS VON, Die Wünschelrute. Ihre magischen Wunderkräfte und die Kunst * * * [The divining rod. Its magic powers and the art * * *], Munich.

1911. HUBER, CARL, Telepathie und Wünschelrute [Telepathy and the divining rod]: Die übersinnliche Welt, 19th year, Berlin.

1911. KLINCKOWSTROEM, Graf CARL VON, Wasserversorgung und Wünschelrute [Water supply and divining rod]: Illustr. Rundschau, 1st year, Hanover.

1911. KLINCKOWSTROEM, Graf CARL VON, Bibliographie der Wünschelrute [Bibliography of the divining rod (with a preface by Aigner)], Munich.

1911. KOCH, K. R., Das Phonendoskop als Wünschelrute [The phonendoscope as a divining rod]: Physikal. Zeitschr., 12th year, Leipzig.

1911. KÖNIG, F., Der Wünschelrute geheimnisvolles Walten—ein Blendwerk [The mysterious action of the divining rod—a delusion]: Ver. Gas- und Wasserf. in Österr.-Ungarn Zeitschr., vol. 51, pp. 36-40, Vienna.

1911. LANZ-LIEBENFELS, J., Theologie und Radiologie [Theology and radiology] Der Türmer, 14th year, Stuttgart.

1911. LOTH, ARTHUR, articles in L'univers, Aug. 24, Aug. 31, Sept. 21, Dec. 28.

1911. LUTTENBACHER, H., Neue Experimente mit der Wünschelrute [New experiments with the divining rod]: Psychische Studien, 38th year, pp. 57-60, Leipzig.

1911. MEYER, G., Die Wünschelrute und ihre Berechtigung [The divining rod and its right]: Ver. Gas- und Wasserf. in Österr.-Ungarn Zeitschr., vol. 51, pp. 148-156, Vienna.

1911. OBST, WALTER, Meine Erfahrungen mit der Wünschelrute [My experiences with the divining rod]: Allgem. Beobachter, 1st year, Hamburg.

1911. PAINE, RALPH D., The book of buried treasure, London, pp. 361-384.

1911. REUSCH, HANS, En ny bok om ønskekvisten [A new book on divining]: Naturen, 35th year, pp. 274-275, Bergen.

1911. ROTH, KARL, Die Wünschelrute auf dem Thermengebiet von Homburg v. d. Höhe [The divining rod in the hot-spring region of Homburg on the Höhe]: Frankfurter Zeit- und Handelsbl., 55th year, Frankfort.

1911. RUPPEL, WILLY, Stunden mit der Wünschelrute [Lessons with the divining rod]: Hildebrandts Zentralbl. Pumpen und Wassertechn., 4th year, Berlin.

1911. Voll, Adam, Die Wünschelrute [The divining rod]: Süddeutsche Monats-hefte, 9th year, pp. 755–758, Munich.

1911. Weber, M., Die Wünschelrute [On the divining rod]: Jour. Gasbeleuchtung und Wasserversorgung, 54th year, pp. 201–203, Munich.

1911. Wertheimer, J., Experiments with water finders: Royal Soc. Arts Jour., vol. 59, pp. 384–389, London.

1911. Wolff, W., Grundwasser und Wünschelrute [Ground water and divining rod]: Deutsche Forstzeitung, vol. 26, Neudamm.

1912. Behrendt, P., Die Versuche mit Rutengängern im Kalibergwerk Riedel bei Hänigsen (Hannover) am 29 September, 1911 [The experiments with diviners in the Riedel potash mine near Hanover on the 29th of September, 1911], Stuttgart.

1912. Birot, Ém., and Roux, Cl., "Hydroscopie et rabdomancie—Généralités—bibliographie," and "Expériences de rabdomancie faites ou à faire à Lyon en 1912 et 1913" [Experiments in rhabdomancy made, or to be made, at Lyon in 1912 and 1913 (with bibliography)]: Soc..d'agr., sci. ind. Lyon An-nales, pp. 129–192.

1912. Bormann, Dr. W., Ferneres über die Wünschelrute [More on the divining rod]: Die übersinnliche Welt, 20th year.

1912. Duclaux, Jacques, La constitution de l'eau [The constitution of water]: Revue générale des sciences, vol. 23, pp. 881–887.

1912. Fehrman, Karl L., Ein Beitrag zur Wünschelrutenfrage [A contribution to the divining-rod question]: Ver. Gas- und Wasserf. in Österr.-Ungarn Zeitschr., vol. 52, Vienna.

1912. Hennig, R., Der Kampf um die Wünschelrute [The dispute over the divining rod]: Natur, 3d year, Leipzig.

1912. Hoernes, R., Die Wünschelrute [The divining rod]: Monatzeit. Österr.-Ungarn, 19th year, Graz.

1912. Klinckowstroem, Graf Carl von, Bibliographie der Wünschelrute seit 1910 und Nächträge [Bibliography of the divining rod since 1910 and addenda]: Schriften Verbands z. Klärung Wünschelrute, part 3, Stuttgart.

1912. Klinckowstroem, Graf Carl von, Die Versuche mit der Wünschelrute im Kalibergwerk Riedel und die Kritik [The experiments with the divining rod in the Riedel potash works and criticism]: Ver. Gas- und Wasserf. in Österr.-Ungarn Zeitschr., vol. 52, Vienna.

1912. Lejeaux, Jean, Le secret des sources [The secret of springs]: Le journal, June 7, Dec. 27.

1912. Lejeaux, Jean, Découvrez vous-même les sources [Discover springs yourself]: La vie à la campagne, Nov. 15.

1912. Mager, Henri, Les moyens de découvrir les eaux souterraines et de les utiliser [The means of finding and utilizing underground water], 775 pp., Paris.

1912. Uslar, Von, Des Landrats von Uslar Arbeiten mit der Wünschelrute in Süd-westafrica [Landrat von Uslar's work with the divining rod in Southwest Africa], Stuttgart.

1912. Vesely, J., Kouzelný Proutek [The rod of divination], Zlata Praha, 29th year, Prague.

1912. Vigen, Charles, La baguette divinatoire en Allemagne. Études récentes [The divining rod in Germany. Recent studies]: La nature, Aug. 17.

1912. Weyrauch, R., Der Begriff des Erfolges bei Arbeiten von Wünschelruten-gängern [The conception of the results of the work of divining-rod operators], Stuttgart.

1913. Birot, Émile, La recherche des eaux souterraines et les sourciers [The investi-gation of ground water and water witches]: Lyon-Colonial, March.

1913. DESCROIX, Two articles on the Congress (of diviners) of 1913 and the experiments in rhabdomancy: L'eau, April.

1913. HÉMON, CAMILLE, La semaine des sourciers [The week of water witches]: Excelsior, Apr. 7.

1913. KLINCKOWSTROEM, Graf. CARL VON, Ergebnisse der Tätigkeit des Landrats von Uslar in Deutschland [Results of the work of the Landrat von Uslar in Germany]: Verbands z. Klärung Wünschelrute Schriften, No. 4.

1913. MAGER, HENRI, Les influences des corps minéraux: Recherche par leurs influences des eaux souterraines, des corps enfouis ou dissimulée, des gisements métallifères [The influence of mineral bodies: Investigation of their influence on underground water, buried or hidden substances, and metalliferous deposits], 236 pp., Paris.

1913. MAGER, HENRI, Les sourciers et leurs procédés: la baguette et le pendule [Water witches and their methods: the divining rod and the magic pendulum], Paris.

1913. MAGER, HENRI, Communication sur les lignes de force susceptibles d'influencer l'homme et d'être enregistrées par une simple baguette [Communication on the lines of force capable of influencing man and of being registered by a simple divining rod], address before the Academy of Science, Apr. 21 and 28.

1913. MARTEL, E.-A., Rapport sur le congrès des baguettisants à Paris en mars 1913, présenté le 7 avril 1913 à la Commission spéciale d'hydrologie souterraine du Ministère de l'agriculture [Report on the congress of diviners at Paris in March, 1913, presented to the special commission of underground hydrology of the Ministry of Agriculture, Apr. 7, 1913].

1913. QUINCY, C., et H. GUILLEMIN, Les sourciers et la baguette divinatoire [The water witches and the divining rod]: Soc. sci. nat. Saône-et-Loire, Bull., vol. 19, pp. 21-28.

1913. RENDU, Dr. JOANN , Rapport sur les trois premières expériences faites par la commission chargée d'étudier la question de la baguette divinatoire, janvier-février, 1913 [Report on the first three experiments made by the commission directed to study the question of the divining rod, January-February, 1913]: Soc. d'agr., sci. ind. Lyon Annales, Travaux de la Commission lyonnaise d'études hydroscopiques, fasc. 3.

1913. ROLLIÈRE, BROTHIER DE, La baguette des sourciers. Classification des faits et des méthodes anciennes et modernes [The divining rod of water witches. Classification of ancient and modern facts and methods].

1913. ROUYER, C., Expérience sur la baguette divinatoire [Experiences with the divining rod]: Soc. sci. nat. Saône-et-Loire, new ser., vol. 19, pp. 51-56.

1913. ROUX, CL., and É. BIROT, La découverte et le captage des eaux souterraines dans le Département du Rhône [The discovery and acquisition of underground waters in the department of the Rhone]: Soc. d'agr., sci. ind. Lyon Annales, 1912, 1913.

1913. VARIGNY, H. DE, Articles sur la baguette et sur le concours des sourciers à Paris en mars, 1913 [Articles on the divining rod and on the congress of water witches at Paris in March, 1913]: Journal des débats, March and April.

1913. VIRE, ARMAND, L'art de découvrir les sources. Les sourciers et la baguette divinatoire [The art of finding springs. Water witches and the divining rod]: La nature, April.

1913. The divining rod in Germany: Harper's Weekly, vol. 57, Feb. 22, p. 22, New York. Discusses revival of faith in divining rod in consequence of drought.

1913. The mystery of the divining rod: Independent, vol. 76, Oct. 9, pp. 64-65, New York.

1913. The divining rod again called into court: Review of Reviews, vol. 48, July, pp. 101-102, New York.

1913. The study of the divining rod: Literary Digest, vol. 46, Feb. 15, p. 341, New York. Translation of an article by E. A. Martel in La nature, Paris, Dec. 21, 1913.

1914. MAGER, HENRI, A new method for the study of mining fields and for finding ore embedded in deep ground. 8 pp. Paris.

1916. SMITH, J. T., The divining rod as an oil finder: Petroleum World, vol. 13, no. 191, p. 371.

PUBLICATIONS NOT DATED.

ANDRIMONT, D', La science hydrologique [The science of hydrology].

Bréviaire du dévin et du sorcier; contenant le traité de la baguette divinatoire; le dragon rouge; les merveilleux secrets du Petit Albert, l'enchiridion du Pape Léon III, etc. [Breviary of the soothsayer and the water finder; treatise on the divining rod; red dragon; secret marvels of Petit Albert, the manual of Pope Leo III, etc.], Paris; figures.

CHALON, P., Recherche et captage des sources [Investigation and development of (underground) springs], 2d ed.

CHILD, S. T., Water finding.

DELEUZE, Histoire critique du magnétisme animal [Critical history of animal magnetism].

DELRIO, Les pratiques superstitieuses de la branche de coudrier [The superstitious uses of the hazel twig], Disquisit. magic, book 3.

ENDRISS, KARL, many articles on the divining rod in German periodicals.

HOLT, HENRY, On the cosmic relations.

JANET, PIERRE, L'automatisme psychologique [Psychological automatism].

RICHET, CHARLES, Les mouvements inconscients [Unconscious movements].

RIOLS, J. DE. See Tournier, Paul.

ROCHAS, A. DE, Effluves odiques [Odic emanations].

TOURNIER, PAUL, L'art de découvrir les sources propres à donner naissance à des fontaines jaillissantes [The art of finding springs capable of giving rise to spouting fountains], Le Bailly, Paris.

INDEX.

DEPARTMENT OF THE INTERIOR
FRANKLIN K. LANE, Secretary

UNITED STATES GEOLOGICAL SURVEY
GEORGE OTIS SMITH, Director

WATER-SUPPLY PAPER 416

THE DIVINING ROD

A HISTORY OF WATER WITCHING

WITH A BIBLIOGRAPHY

BY

ARTHUR J. ELLIS

WASHINGTON
GOVERNMENT PRINTING OFFICE
1917

DATE DUE

1CO 38-297